McGraw-Hill Education

500 SAT
Reading, Writing and
Language Questions

to Know by Test Day

Star Corea

McGraw-Hill Education

500 SAT Reading, Writing and Language Questions

to Know by Test Day

Second Edition

Anaxos, Inc.

New York   Chicago   San Francisco   Athens   London
Madrid   Mexico City   Milan   New Delhi
Singapore   Sydney   Toronto

1 2 3 4 5 6 7 8 9   QFR/QFR   23 22 21 20 19 18

ISBN   978-1-260-13553-4
MHID   1-260-13553-5

e-ISBN   978-1-260-13554-1
e-MHID   1-260-13554-3

SAT is a registered trademark of the College Board, which was not involved in the production of, and does not endorse, this product.

Anaxos, Inc. has been creating education and reference materials for over fifteen years. Based in Austin, Texas, the company uses writers from across the globe who offer expertise on an array of subjects just as expansive.

McGraw-Hill Education products are available at special quantity discounts to use as premiums and sales promotions or for use in corporate training programs. To contact a representative, please visit the Contact Us pages at www.mhprofessional.com.

CONTENTS

INTRODUCTION

Congratulations! You've taken a big step toward SAT success by purchasing *McGraw-Hill Education 500 Reading, Writing and Language Questions to Know by Test Day.* We are here to help you take the next step and score high on your SAT exam so you can get into the college or university of your choice!

This book gives you 500 SAT-style multiple-choice questions that cover all the most essential reading and writing material. The questions will give you valuable independent practice to supplement your regular textbook and the ground you have already covered in your English and reading class. Each question is clearly explained in the answer key.

This book and the others in the series were written by expert teachers who know the SAT inside and out and can identify crucial information as well as the kinds of questions that are most likely to appear on the exam.

You might be the kind of student who needs to study extra a few weeks before the exam for a final review. Or you might be the kind of student who puts off preparing until the last minute before the exam. No matter what your preparation style, you will benefit from reviewing these 500 questions, which closely parallel the content, format, and degree of difficulty of the Reading, Writing and Language questions on the actual SAT exam. These questions and the explanations in the answer key are the ideal last-minute study tool for those final weeks before the test.

If you practice with all the questions and answers in this book, we are certain you will build the skills and confidence needed to excel on the SAT. Good luck!

—*Editors of McGraw-Hill Education*

PART 1

Critical Reading

CHAPTER 1

Set 1 Critical Reading Questions

Passage 1

Many forms of prejudice exist in society today. Not all forms of prejudice are obvious to the average person. "Benevolent prejudice" is a type of discrimination that often seems friendly or harmless. There are no outward signs of anger, fear, or violence, but it is still an unjustified or incorrect attitude toward a person based on his or her social group.

An example of benevolent racism is the assumption that black Americans are all athletic, musical, religious, or have strong family bonds. These qualities are positive, but the misconception that they apply to all black Americans is a form of prejudice. Another form of benevolent prejudice is related to society's attitude toward women. When people believe all women are weaker than men, are natural mothers, are more caring and compassionate, or should not work as hard as men at a job, they are being sexist.

One of the most insidious forms of prejudice is discrimination against the elderly, which often takes the form of older people being marginalized or patronized out of pity. People will often speak to the elderly in a slow, infantile manner, or they will assume that the senior citizen is a needy, nonproductive member of society. There are several forms of age-related bias, or ageism. The elderly are often seen as bungling and ineffectual, and are therefore treated differently, despite there being absolutely no proof of ineptitude.

Ageism toward the elderly often manifests itself in the workplace. An older job applicant may be passed over for a younger one purely on the basis of age—because the older person is viewed as less capable, not because of an actual lack of experience or skills. At the other end of the spectrum, a company may try to coerce a long-time employee to go into retirement before he or she is ready, in order to pay a new person less money to do the same job. It may be assumed that an older person would not want to adapt to new ideas or use a new technology, or that possible medical issues could impact job performance or attendance.

These issues are not mutually exclusive to older people. They could affect a person of any age. Because of benevolent ageism, many reliable, responsible senior citizens are losing jobs and being forced out of work.

1. Which of the following statements is *not* supported by the passage?
   - (A) Ageism is discrimination against individuals or groups because of their age.
   - (B) Women also experience forms of benevolent prejudice.
   - (C) Many companies refuse to hire workers younger than age eighteen.
   - (D) Ageism is frequently seen in the workforce.

2. The word *ineptitude* in line 19 most nearly means
   - (A) "reluctance."
   - (B) "divulgence."
   - (C) "incompetence."
   - (D) "omnipotence."

3. According to the passage, benevolent prejudice
   - (A) appears friendly and harmless.
   - (B) is easy to recognize.
   - (C) is not as serious as hostile prejudice.
   - (D) should be taken as a compliment.

4. Which of the following statements is true about ageism?
   - (A) The term *sexism* was coined in the mid-twentieth century.
   - (B) John McCain didn't win the presidency because he was too old.
   - (C) There is more than one kind of age-related bias.
   - (D) Companies are allowed to promote the retirement of older workers.

5. The word *manifests* in line 20 most nearly means
   - (A) "admires."
   - (B) "reveals."
   - (C) "abominates."
   - (D) "relinquishes."

6. All of the following statements are not true *except*
   - (A) an older person would not want to adapt to new ideas or use technology.
   - (B) elderly people have more medical issues that keep them out of work.
   - (C) older workers lack the experience and skills to be able to perform as well as young employees.
   - (D) there are some jobs that could be too physically demanding for an elderly employee.

7. The word *insidious* in line 13 most nearly means

   (A) "transparent."
   (B) "sinister."
   (C) "misappropriated."
   (D) "benevolent."

8. The author's attitude toward ageism can best be described as

   (A) appalled.
   (B) delighted.
   (C) transcendental.
   (D) abrogated.

9. The second paragraph mostly serves to

   (A) define *prejudice*.
   (B) give examples of benevolent prejudice.
   (C) provide reasons prejudice is hurtful.
   (D) compare and contrast hostile and benevolent prejudice.

10. All of the following statements about the author's purpose are true *except*

   (A) to show readers that not all forms of prejudice are negative.
   (B) to bring attention to a form of prejudice people may be unaware of.
   (C) to convince employers to hire elderly workers.
   (D) to illustrate how everyone can have the same problems in the workplace.

Passage 2

A mysterious ailment called colony collapse disorder (CCD) has wiped out large numbers of honeybees. CCD is when all of the worker bees who produce the honey leave the hive. Only the queen, a few nurse bees that care for the immature bees, and a food supply are left. With no drone bees to create more food and build up the hive, it eventually dies. The exact cause of the problem is as yet unknown, but there are a number of theories. Recent studies have revealed that there is likely more than one factor affecting the bees, rather than a single cause.

Many experts believe that the colonies may have been hit by viral or fungal infections. Bees' number-one stressor is the varroa mite, a parasite that depletes the blood supply of drone bees and bee larvae. This weakens the developing bees and shortens their life expectancy. It also causes deformities in the bees, like missing legs or wings.

Other possible causes of bee attrition include malnutrition from a lack of nutrients and food sources, poison by fertilizers and pesticides, habitat loss due to deforestation and increased agriculture, and a loss of genetic diversity as a result of commercial breeding. Climate change also impacts bee health because it disrupts plant growth cycles. If the plants and the bees are not synced, the bees may try to pollinate at the wrong times, when the plants have not produced enough pollen.

The loss of these bees is both an environmental and economic disaster. Bees pollinate one-third of all food produced, which includes 70 different types of crops. Six thousand tons of honey is produced every year. If bee colonies die off, all of these crops would have to be pollinated by hand, which would cost millions of dollars in labor. This means that many of the common foods that we consume, including fruits and almonds, could become so rare that they would become luxuries rather than diet staples. Bees are also responsible for the pollination of numerous plants in the wild. This symbiotic relationship means that if the bees disappear permanently, so will the wild plants that depend on them to reproduce, leading to a collapse of many ecosystems.

11. With which of the following statements would the author most likely agree?

   (A) Professional and amateur beekeepers are affected by CCD, as are stationary and migratory populations in the wild.
   (B) Even before CCD, honeybees suffered from a number of ailments that affected the numbers in their populations.
   (C) There are no patterns of loss in the affected populations.
   (D) Researchers believe that there is a single cause of CCD, rather than several.

12. All of the following are possible causes of CCD *except* that

   (A) the honeybees are being harmed by human-made substances, such as pesticides.
   (B) the pollination of luxury crops keeps bees from pollinating wild plants.
   (C) commercial breeding may be causing reproductive problems and genetic mutations.
   (D) the honeybee's natural defenses may be lowered by poor nutrition.

13. The word *attrition* in line 14 most nearly means

   (A) "attraction."
   (B) "reduction."
   (C) "fatality."
   (D) "increase."

14. It can be inferred from the first paragraph that

    (A) it is more important that we solve the economic consequences than that we worry about the environmental effects of CCD.

    (B) CCD is caused by humans altering the environments they live in with flowers and plant species that are not indigenous.

    (C) the causes of CCD are complex, which is why research has shown that one single trigger is not a likely scenario.

    (D) only commonly consumed food crops are affected by CCD, not specialty foods.

15. The "symbiotic relationship" of bees and plants (line XX) is analogous to

    (A) elephants and antelopes that share the same watering hole during the hot summer months in Africa.

    (B) cleaner shrimp that feed off the bacteria living on bigger fish that would otherwise make the bigger fish sick.

    (C) tapeworms that enter the intestinal tracts of mammals and feed off the host until it dies.

    (D) the larval stage of insects before metamorphosis into adulthood.

16. In the last paragraph, the word *staples* most likely refers to

    (A) the connection between the plants from pollination.

    (B) common foods we eat.

    (C) unique foods that are eaten on special occasions.

    (D) food that are low in calories for diets.

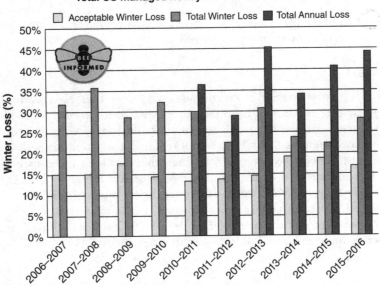

Total US managed honeybee colonies Loss Estimates

https://beeinformed.org/2016/05/10/nations-beekeepers-lost-44-percent-of-bees-in-2015-16/

17. All of the following statements could be considered "acceptable winter loss" conditions *except*

    (A) the winter season was much colder than expected.
    (B) the hive was destroyed by snowplows.
    (C) there was not enough food for bees to store for the winter.
    (D) the hive suffered from CCD.

18. Based on the graph, what is the *overall* trend seen in bee colony losses from 2006–2016?

    (A) It stays pretty much the same.
    (B) There is no trend; the numbers are totally random.
    (C) There is a general increase in all loss amounts.
    (D) The most loss happens in the wintertime.

19. Prior to 2010–2011, the graph does not include a column for total annual loss. It can be inferred that

    (A) there was no way to measure how many bees died in a year.
    (B) bees only died in winter.
    (C) no one cared how many bees died because they were a nuisance.
    (D) scientists realized there were other causes for the loss of bees in addition to winter.

20. Looking at the graph, the author of the passage would most likely agree that

    (A) the increase in total annual deaths is caused by CCD.
    (B) the increase in total annual deaths mean there are more toxins being used in the environment.
    (C) little change in winter loss means some other factor is killing the bees.
    (D) bees can only survive in warm weather.

Passage 3

It was a dull New England town; no one could deny that, for everybody was so intensely proper and well-born that nobody dared to be jolly. All the houses were square, aristocratic mansions with Revolutionary elms in front and spacious coach-houses behind. The knockers had a supercilious perk to their bronze or brass noses—as though they knew they had been there since the war for independence—the dandelions on the lawns had a highly connected air, and the very pigs were evidently descended from "our first families." Stately dinner-parties, decorous dances, moral picnics, and much teapot gossiping were the social resources of the place. Of course, the young people flirted, for that diversion is apparently irradicable even in the "best society," but it was done with a propriety that was edifying to behold.

One can easily imagine that such a starched state of things would not be particularly attractive to a travelled young gentleman like Lennox, who, as Kate very truly said, had been spoilt by the flattery, luxury, and gayety of foreign society. He did his best, but by the end of the first week ennui claimed him for its own, and passive endurance was all that was left him. From perfect despair he was rescued by the scarlet stockings, which went tripping by one day as he stood at the window, planning some means of escape.

A brisk, blithe-faced girl passed in a gray walking suit with a distracting pair of high-heeled boots and glimpses of scarlet at the ankle. Modest, perfectly so, I assure you, were the glimpses; but the feet were so decidedly pretty that one forgot to look at the face appertaining thereunto. It wasn't a remarkably lovely face, but it was a happy, wholesome one, with all sorts of good little dimples in cheek and chin, sunshiny twinkles in the black eyes, and a decided, yet lovable look about the mouth that was quite satisfactory. A busy, bustling little body she seemed to be, for sack-pockets and muff were full of bundles, and the trim boots tripped briskly over the ground, as if the girl's heart were as light as her heels. Somehow this active, pleasant figure seemed to wake up the whole street, and leave a streak of sunshine behind it, for every one nodded as it passed, and the primmest faces relaxed into smiles, which lingered when the girl had gone.

"Uncommonly pretty feet—she walks well, which American girls seldom do— all waddle or prance—nice face, but the boots are French, and it does my heart good to see them." Lennox made these observations to himself as the young lady approached, nodded to Kate at another window, gave a quick but comprehensive glance at himself and trotted round the corner, leaving the impression on his mind that a whiff of fresh spring air had blown through the street in spite of the December snow. He didn't trouble himself to ask who it was, but fell into the way of lounging in the bay-window at about three PM, and watching the gray and scarlet figure pass with its blooming cheeks, bright eyes, and elastic step. Having nothing else to do, he took to petting this new whim, and quite depended on the daily stirring-up that the sight of the energetic damsel gave him. Kate saw it all, but took no notice. She was as soft as a summer sea, and by some clever stroke had Belle Morgan to tea that very week.

For the first time in his life, the "Crusher," as his male friends called him, got crushed; for Belle, with the subtle skill of a quick-witted, keen-sighted girl, soon saw and condemned the elegant affectations which others called foreign polish.

21. Which of the following statements most accurately describes the purpose of the first paragraph?

   (A) To mollify the reader before exploring some uncomfortable subjects
   (B) To describe in detail the type of world that Belle Morgan stepped into
   (C) To emphasize the differences between Kate and Belle
   (D) To imply that the town had been brought to life by Lennox's presence

22. As used in line 4, the word "supercilious" most nearly means

    (A) "humble."
    (B) "pompous."
    (C) "diplomatic."
    (D) "implacable."

23. In line 7, the expression "our first families" is analogous to

    (A) the British colonists of the Americas.
    (B) German Hessian soldiers in America.
    (C) the noble families from Spain in the Americas.
    (D) the descendants of Adam and Eve.

24. As used in line 8, the word *decorous* most nearly means

    (A) "mendacious."
    (B) "inexhaustible."
    (C) "tenuous."
    (D) "well-behaved."

25. The narrator uses the clause "ennui claimed him for its own" to mean that

    (A) Lennox was immensely bored by the end of the first week.
    (B) Lennox and Kate had gone on a vacation together.
    (C) Kate and Belle were both trying to marry Lennox.
    (D) Belle was Lennox's new guardian.

26. It can be inferred from the passage that

    (A) Kate and Lennox went to the same school in Boston.
    (B) Kate and Belle had been best friends since childhood.
    (C) Belle and Lennox met previously during the summertime.
    (D) Belle was the girl in the scarlet stockings.

27. As used in line 10, the word "irradicable" most nearly means

    (A) "assiduous."
    (B) "entrenched."
    (C) "saccharine."
    (D) "untoward."

28. According to the passage, Belle can be described by all of the following words *except*

    (A) *blithe.*
    (B) *wholesome.*
    (C) *pleasant.*
    (D) *meager.*

29. According to lines 28–30, which of the following statements best describes Belle's effect on people in the street?

(A) She angered the high-society ladies, who saw her as impertinent.

(B) She exemplified all of the attributes that made the town so dull.

(C) She enchanted and delighted everyone she passed.

(D) She repulsed everyone because she looked like an ogre.

30. As used in line 39, the word *elastic* most nearly means

(A) "accusatory."

(B) "flexible."

(C) "sedentary."

(D) "quotidian."

31. In lines 33–36, the author suggests that Belle's presence

(A) has no effect on anyone in the town.

(B) must come to an end soon.

(C) has been detrimental to Kate.

(D) is a complete contrast to her surroundings.

32. Which of the following statements best describe(s) the reason why the narrator calls Belle "a busy, bustling little body" in line 25?

I. She was walking briskly to an unknown destination.

II. Her clothes implied that she was a nurse.

III. Her hands and pockets were full of packages.

(A) I

(B) I and II

(C) III

(D) I and III

33. In lines 44–46, the narrator suggests that

(A) Belle gets out of school every day at three PM.

(B) Kate is jealous of Belle's rosy complexion.

(C) Lennox watches Belle pass by his window every day at three PM.

(D) Belle is a dancer in the local ballet company.

34. It can be inferred from the last paragraph that

(A) Kate and Belle had become mortal enemies over their affections for Lennox.

(B) Lennox was usually the heartbreaker, but this time a girl had caught his heart.

(C) Belle was immediately accepted by the town's society.

(D) Belle was from Europe, which immediately made her more attractive to Lennox.

35. As used in line 46, the word *affectations* most nearly means

(A) "derivatives."

(C) "rejuvenation."

χ (D) "mannerisms."

(E) "disillusions."

Passage 4A

More than 150 years passed from the signing of the Declaration of Independence to the establishment of the National Archives Building in 1934. During the interim, a deficit of proper, secure storage resulted in the loss of priceless information. Many documents were stolen or destroyed over the years. One such significant loss was the 1890 United States census records.

The 1890 census was unique in several ways. It was the first time an electrical tabulation system would be used to calculate results. It was also the first time each family would receive its own record and included inquiries regarding race, home ownership, primary language spoken, immigration, and naturalization. It also asked questions related to the Civil War.

But the 1890 census was also fraught with complaints and political intrigue. New York officials were accused of inflating numbers. A complaint by St. Paul, Minnesotan businessmen led to 19 indictments against Minneapolis businessmen for falsifying 1,100 names on their census counts. Further investigations were brought to a halt when a fire destroyed most of the 1890 census records in 1921. Had these records survived, we would have inimitable information on these issues, as well as on American industrialization, westward migration, veteran services, and other characteristics of the American population at that time.

The data would have been incredibly enlightening and useful in limitless applications—to historians, political scientists, and so on—but they are now completely lost to history. It is really quite remarkable that so many valuable records even exist today. Unfortunately, it wasn't until the twentieth century that the government became vigilant and proactive about the safety and preservation of historical records.

Passage 4B

The National Archives Building was approved by Congress and President Franklin D. Roosevelt in 1934 for the preservation and care of documents and records of national significance. Previously, these records had been stored in a variety of basements, sheds, business, and storage facilities, with no security in place to protect documents from theft or environmental damage.

Until the end of the nineteenth century, there was little interest in creating this type of facility. But the fire that destroyed the Commerce Building in 1921 and resulted in the loss of the 1890 census records spurred many historians and archivists into action. In 1934, Congress created the National Historical

Publications Commission to oversee the protection and preservation of documents that were not stored in the National Archives Building.

One of the tenets of democracy is that the government must answer to the people. The National Archives Building exists to provide a centralized system to the American people to access information that can hold the government accountable. The National Archives Building currently has over 40 facilities nationwide, including field archives, federal records centers, presidential libraries, the Federal Register, and the National Historical Publications and Records Commission. Its mission is "to safeguard and preserve the records of our government, ensure that the people can discover, use, and learn from this documentary heritage, and ensure continuing access to the essential documentation of the rights of American citizens and the actions of their government." The Electronic Records Archive has the responsibility of protecting and storing information for a digital age. It provides instantaneous access to millions of documents, videos, graphs, and photos, but is still no replacement for preserving the original inspirational founding documents on display in our nation's capital.

36. As used in line 3, the word *deficit* most nearly means

(A) "abundance."
(B) "scarcity."
(C) "anonymous."
(D) "flammable."

37. The author describes the records of the 1890 census as "inimitable" because

(A) the format was modeled on the censuses being used in Europe.
(B) they would have given us unique, reliable insights into nineteenth-century American life.
(C) we could have used them to formulate current immigration law.
(D) they are the only US census records with information about Abraham Lincoln's family.

38. Based on the passages, all of the following are true about the 1890 census *except*

(A) individual families obtained their own records.
(B) it was used to learn about Civil War veterans.
(C) it was unlike prior ones.
(D) it was printed in a number of languages.

39. As used in Passage 4A, the word *vigilant* most nearly means

(A) "protracted."
(B) "mawkish."
(C) "superficial."
(D) "attentive."

40. Which of the following statements best supports the author's conclusion in Passage 4A?

(A) A special building where archives could be properly stored was built in 1930.

(B) The 1890 census was the first to use punch cards.

(C) America's historical records were completely ignored in the twentieth century.

(D) A large number of census schedules are incomplete.

41. The author's purpose in Passage 4B is to

(A) reveal where the United States government stores its top-secret information.

(B) explain why it is important to save important historical documents.

(C) give a brief history of the National Archives Building and what it does.

(D) convince tourists to visit the National Archives Building on their vacations.

42. In paragraph 2 of Passage 4B, the word *spurred* most nearly means

(A) "precipitated."

(B) "incited."

(C) "daunted."

(D) "refined."

43. The authors of both passages would agree on all of the following *except*

(A) the loss of historical documents is a tragedy.

(B) the fire in 1921 was the main factor in creating the National Archives Building.

(C) now that records can be stored electronically, paper records are no longer important.

(D) American citizens have a right to access information about their country and government.

44. People might use the National Archives Building to

I. research their family's immigration history.

II. obtain military benefits.

III. find out where elected officials have their bank accounts.

IV. read documents related to the founding of this country.

(A) I only

(B) IV only

(C) I and II

(D) I and III

45. After reading the final paragraph of Passage 4B, it can be inferred that the author feels

(A) saving all these old papers is pointless.

(B) the best way to preserve historical documents is to scan them electronically and get rid of the originals to save space.

(C) viewing the Declaration of Independence and the Constitution in person is the best way to see these inspiring documents.

(D) there are too many different locations, making it difficult to find the documents you are looking for.

Passage 5A

During World War II, sending and receiving codes required hours of encrypting and decrypting. The Japanese used their considerable skill as code breakers to intercept many messages being sent by American forces in the Pacific.

In an effort to find quicker and more secure ways to send and receive communications, the United States enlisted Navajo Indians to relay critical information between military units. The Navajo language was chosen in part because of its complex grammatical structure and syntax. In addition, it was still an unwritten language at that time and was spoken only on the Navajo lands of the American Southwest. As a result, the use of the Navajo language as a code was a remarkable success. Crucial battles, including the famous Battle of Iwo Jima, were successful because of the use of the Navajo code. And after the war, Japan's chief of intelligence admitted they were never able to break it.

It is estimated that more than 400 Navajos served in this program, which remained highly classified until 1968. The code talkers returned home without fanfare after the war and were sworn to secrecy about the code's existence. For decades, the American people had no idea that the US triumph in the Pacific theater was partly because of these courageous men. Luckily, the exploits of these heroic soldiers are finally making their way into mainstream American history.

Passage 5B

Thanks to recent Hollywood movies and TV documentaries, when you mention code talkers, most people today immediately think of the now-legendary bilingual Navajo soldiers recruited during World War II. But, in fact, this type of code talking did not begin in that war, and Navajo was not the first language used.

The original code talkers were Choctaw Indians from southeastern Oklahoma, and it was their language that was first utilized near the end of World War I. It is said that an American officer got the idea to use Choctaw while serving in France. Overhearing a couple of Choctaw Indians in his company speaking to each other in their native language, he supposed that it would likely make an unbreakable code that the US Army could use to get information past the Germans. His hunch proved to be correct. Choctaw soldiers were soon placed in each company, and Choctaw was spoken over radio waves.

Although the Navajo code talkers are the most famous, Navajo was not even the only Native American language used during World War II. Choctaw was also used, in addition to other languages, such as Cherokee, Lakota Meskwaki, and Comanche. The Navajo received recognition from Congress in 2000 for their contributions. But clearly the Choctaw deserved praise as well for their valor and dedication. Finally, in 2013, a bill was passed honoring the 33 tribes who had sent code talkers to the battlefields. Unfortunately, none of the Choctaw that had been in WWI were still alive to attend, but their children were.

46. Which of the following statements can be inferred from Passage 5A?

(A) The lack of military terminology in the original Navajo vocabulary was an obstacle.

(B) Maintaining secrecy is vital to the national security of every country, particularly in wartime.

(C) The Navajo language was successful because few people in the world could understand it.

(D) Native Americans had successfully sent secure messages in previous wars, such as World War I.

47. The main point of Passage 5B is that

(A) although the Navajo soldiers are the most renowned, they were not the original code talkers.

(B) the representations of Choctaw Indians in movies and on TV are inaccurate.

(C) the now-legendary Navajos recruited during World War II were not bilingual.

(D) the Cherokee, Lakota Meskwaki, and Comanche languages were better codes.

48. The author of Passage 5A mentions the admission by the Japanese chief of intelligence in order to

(A) provide an example of the tensions between the Allied and Axis powers.

(B) highlight the friendship between the United States and Japan.

(C) imply that the Japanese may have been lying about not breaking the code.

(D) emphasize just how successful the use of Navajo was as a code.

49. As used in paragraph 2 of Passage 5B, the word *hunch* most nearly means

(A) "aspersion."

(B) "domesticity."

(C) "intuition."

(D) "meditation."

50. Which of the following statements most accurately describes the relationship between Passage 5A and Passage 5B?

    (A) Passage 5A is a direct rebuttal of the ideas in Passage 5B.
    (B) Both passages arrive at the same conclusion through different analyses.
    (C) Passage 5B provides an alternative perspective to the topic introduced in Passage 5A.
    (D) The passages address similar aspects of the same topic but arrive at different conclusions.

51. As used in paragraph 3 of Passage 5A, the word *exploits* most nearly means

    (A) "unimpaired conditions."
    (B) "causes of distress."
    (C) "courageous acts."
    (D) "harsh denunciations."

52. Which of the following most accurately describes the purpose of paragraph 1 in Passage 5B?

    (A) To criticize the portrayal of Native Americans in Hollywood
    (B) To explain the renown of Navajo code talkers in society today
    (C) To exemplify the bravery of the Choctaw soldiers
    (D) To justify the use of real languages as military code

53. The author of Passage 5B would most likely respond to the conclusion of Passage 5A by pointing out that

    (A) Native American languages were unwritten.
    (B) Choctaw soldiers still do not receive the same recognition as Navajo soldiers.
    (C) the Battle of Iwo Jima would have been lost without the use of the Navajo code.
    (D) the Choctaw War Memorial was not erected until 1995.

54. As used in paragraph 3 of Passage 5A, the word *fanfare* most nearly means

    (A) "camaraderie."
    (B) "celebration."
    (C) "pantomime."
    (D) "orthodoxy."

55. The author of Passage 5B implies in paragraph 2 that

    (A) although Choctaw was used openly, it was never deciphered by the Germans.
    (B) the British used the Welsh language to send messages between military units.
    (C) the Choctaw did not refer to themselves as code talkers.
    (D) the Choctaw soldiers in World War I never received a medal of honor.

56. It can be inferred from the passages that both authors would agree that

(A) the US Army owes many victories to the Native American code talkers.

(B) Navajo was spoken only on the Navajo lands of the American Southwest.

(C) code talkers memorized all the terms because codebooks could not be taken into the field.

(D) informal, shortcut code words were essential to getting a quick response.

57. With which of the following statements would the author of Passage 5A most likely agree?

(A) The code talkers used symbolism for military terms not used in Navajo, such as *grenade*.

(B) The idea to use Navajo was discussed by generals during the Spanish-American War.

(C) Navajo code talkers are overrated and should remain in obscurity.

(D) Navajo was the most successful military code in modern history.

58. As used in paragraph 2 of Passage 5B, the word *company* refers to

(A) a theater group.

(B) a ballet troupe.

(C) a military unit.

(D) houseguests.

Passage 6

According to a recent report, rates in the United States are diminishing for both the diagnoses of new cancers, also known as incidence, and the death rate for all cancers combined. This is true for both men and women, especially in the most frequent cancers among men (lung, colon, and prostate) and women (breast and colon). Cancer death rates declined by 13 percent between 2004 and 2013. Forty percent of reported cancer cases are linked to tobacco use. However, the lung cancer death rate varies dramatically between states and regions.

Deviation in smoking pervasiveness is influenced by several factors, including public awareness of the harm of tobacco use, tolerance of tobacco use within the community, local tobacco control activities, and local promotional activities by the tobacco industry. The states where lung cancer death rates for women are on the rise have higher percentages of adult female smokers, low taxes on tobacco products, and local economies that have been dependent on tobacco farming and production for generations.

Men and women continue to have higher incidence and death rates in areas where tobacco use is deeply rooted in daily life, stated the director of the North American Association of Central Cancer Registries. Tobacco farming regions like the South and Midwest have the highest rates of smokers. The geographic disparity in smoking-related cancers is therefore due mostly to behaviors, not environmental factors such as exposure to pollutants or chemicals, she added. West Virginia has the highest rate of female smokers and no laws banning smoking in any public places. It also has the lowest tobacco taxes in the country.

In contrast, California was the first state to implement a statewide tobacco control program that includes high taxes and laws against smoking in public places, such as restaurants and city parks, to reduce exposure to secondhand smoke. And it was one of the only two states, in addition to Utah, to show declines in both lung cancer incidence and deaths in women. The report also draws a comparison between lung and skin cancers, which are both firmly influenced by behavior.

Other highly encouraging findings revealed by the report include decreases in incidence and death rates in nearly all racial and ethnic groups. CDC reports overall smoking trends have decreased from 21 percent in 2005 to 15 percent in 2015. Once again, states with targeted programs have better results.

All these achievements, however, must be seen as a starting point rather than a destination. A dual effort regarding the inextricable link between smoking and cancer and targeted anti-smoking campaigns, as well as ongoing research to improve prevention, early detection, and treatment of cancers, will be needed to augment this progress into the future.

59. It can be inferred from the passage that

   (A) progress is being made against all cancers, in particular the most common types.
   (B) more needs to be done to lower the incidence and death rates from cancer in certain ethnic groups.
   (C) death rates for all smoking-related cancers are on the rise for women.
   (D) most states have vigorous tobacco control programs.

60. As used in line 1, the word *diminishing* most nearly means

   (A) "aspiring."
   (B) "exasperating."
   (C) "vindicating."
   (D) "shrinking."

61. Which of the following statements does the passage support?

   (A) Changes in incidence can be caused by changes in screening practices.
   (B) The regional differences in lung cancer trends highlight the success of tobacco control programs.
   (C) Smoking accounts for approximately 40 percent of all cancer deaths.
   (D) There is not a lot of variation in tobacco smoking patterns across the United States.

62. The second paragraph mostly serves to

(A) explain why different states and regions have different lung cancer death rates.

(B) recommend new local tobacco control activities.

(C) dissuade women from working in restaurants and city parks.

(D) warn against tobacco farming and production.

63. As used in paragraph 2, the word *pervasiveness* most nearly means

(A) "corrosiveness."

(B) "ubiquity."

(C) "resilience."

(D) "opulence."

64. The primary purpose of the passage is to

(A) reveal that science cannot detect differences between cancer cells.

(B) question the differences in cancer incidence and death rates between racial and ethnic groups.

(C) provide an update on cancer trends, specifically smoking-related lung cancer.

(D) discuss trends in cancer treatment options in the United States.

65. All of the following are supported by explicit statements in the passage *except*

(A) underserved, low-income cancer patients must be served in the communities where they live.

(B) we must accelerate and improve our efforts in reducing the burden of cancer in this country.

(C) lung cancer continues to rob many people of a long, healthy life because of tobacco use.

(D) the decline in incidences and mortality is evidence of real gains in prevention, early detection, and treatment.

66. The conclusion implies which of the following statements?

(A) Efforts in prevention, early detection, and treatment should be frequently assessed and enhanced.

(B) Cancer death rates have been plummeting since the first report was released.

(C) This is the first concurrent decline in cancer incidence for both men and women.

(D) Decreases in incidence and death rates are being seen across the board.

67. Which of the following could be another example of the "environmental factors" mentioned in paragraph 3?

  (A) Pollution from automobiles
  (B) High-stress workplace
  (C) Long travel hours
  (D) Wildlife preservation

68. As used in the last sentence, the word *augment* most nearly means to

  (A) "converge."
  (B) "advance."
  (C) "wrangle."
  (D) "expand."

State	New Incidences of Cancer 2017	Estimated Cancer Deaths 2017	Smoking Population 2016
California	176,140	59,400	11.0%
Utah	10,990	3,180	8.8%
West Virginia	11,690	4,780	24.8%
Florida	124,740	43,870	15.5%

69. Based on the table, the data supports which of the following statements?

  (A) California and Utah populations have the lowest percentage of smokers.
  (B) Southern states have the highest reported new incidences of cancer.
  (C) West Virginia has the highest percentage of cancer-related deaths and the highest percentage of smokers.
  (D) California and Utah have the lowest percentage of cancer-related deaths.

70. Which of the following data would the author most likely *not* use to support his argument?

  (A) West Virginia's smoking population percentage and estimated cancer-related deaths are the highest.
  (B) Utah's smoking population percentage and estimated cancer-related deaths are the lowest.
  (C) California's highest reported new incidences and the second lowest smoking population percentage.
  (D) Florida has the second highest smoking population percentage and the second highest estimated cancer-related deaths.

Passage 7

The human body creates a lot of heat. In addition to that which we create by running or jumping, we constantly use energy on involuntary functions such as blinking or blood circulation. These types of processes must go on at all times in the body, without our control, even during sleep. But unlike reptiles, which use only outside sources to heat and cool their bodies, mammals maintain a consistent temperature. Therefore, heat must be controlled by a source from the outside environment or from our own bodily functions.

The part of your brain that tells the body it is overheating is called the hypothalamus. The hypothalamus is a gland that helps regulate the body and maintain homeostasis. It causes a person to shiver when the body temperature drops or to sweat when the body temperature rises. The body performs at its optimum when it maintains a constant body temperature.

The cooling process is controlled by the circulatory system. The body disperses heat into the air by exhaling warm, humidified air and by evaporating sweat. The evaporation of sweat cools both the skin and the blood in the vessels beneath it. This blood then returns to your core, cooling your internal body temperature.

These processes work best when the ambient temperature is around 70 degrees. It begins to become less efficient when the temperature starts to match our core body temperature of 98 degrees. This can cause dehydration, leading to an inability to sweat due to hot, dry conditions. It also does not work as well when the humidity in the air rises, as the rate of evaporation slows down. That's when you begin to feel hot and uncomfortable.

Dangers of overheating range from mild to severe. Mild symptoms include dizziness, headaches, muscle weakness, red skin, and fatigue. More serious implications include heat stroke, nausea and vomiting, painful cramps, and eventually organ failure.

71. All of the following statements can be inferred from the passage *except*

    (A) to reduce energy costs, air-conditioning systems should be turned on only when the room's temperature rises above 70 degrees.
    (B) heat is a byproduct of work being done by the body.
    (C) because of the nature of our body's temperature control mechanism, we need a cooler ambient temperature for it to function optimally.
    (D) humidity has a significant effect because it interferes with the evaporation of sweat.

72. Based on the information in lines 2–4, another example of an "involuntary function" performed by the human body could include

    (A) chewing.
    (B) walking.
    (C) breathing.
    (D) sniffing.

73. The author mentions reptiles in lines 4–5 in order to

(A) suggest that humans and reptiles share many evolutionary traits.
(B) emphasize the importance of temperature regulation for all living things.
(C) provide a comparison in the way that different species deal with temperature changes.
(D) imply that reptilian temperature regulation is superior to that of humans.

74. In paragraph 2, the word *homeostasis* most likely means

(A) "human body function."
(B) "a condition when the body gets too cold."
(C) "maintaining a constant condition."
(D) "biological air-conditioning."

75. The "core" described in paragraph 3 is most analogous to the body's

(A) system.
(B) center.
(C) extremities.
(D) molecules.

76. The purpose of paragraphs 2 and 3 is to

(A) explain how the circulatory system works.
(B) show how blocking sweat can cause heat stroke.
(C) changes explain how to prevent hypothermia.
(D) illustrate the body's natural protections from temperature.

77. As used in paragraph 4, the word *ambient* most nearly means

(A) "surrounding."
(B) "botanical."
(C) "stoic."
(D) "punctilious."

78. A person exhibiting the following symptoms might be suffering from mild overheating.

I. An upset stomach
II. Headache
III. Vomiting
IV. Dizziness

(A) II only
(B) I and III
(C) II and IV
(D) I, II, and IV

79. In paragraph 3, the word *disperse* most nearly means

(A) "diffuse."
(B) "disintegrate."
(C) "divide."
(D) "dissolve."

80. The author's purpose for this passage is most likely

(A) to describe cures for overheating.
(B) to illustrate how the body maintains the same temperature in all conditions.
(C) to compare how different species cool themselves through different methods.
(D) to explain the body's natural cooling system and the dangers of overheating.

Passage 8A

The image of women during wartime is primarily based on their presence on the home front, not on the front lines. Women were banned from enlistment in the US military until well into the twentieth century, and until January 2013 were not permitted to serve in active combat.

Yet some women did not allow that restriction to stop them from fighting on either the Union or Confederate side during the Civil War, even though both armies also prohibited their enlistment. Because it was illegal for them to fight on the battlefield, these brave and unconventional women embedded themselves in the army camps by concealing their gender. They changed their names and disguised themselves as men in order to become soldiers. Once enlisted and in the camps, it was crucial to act and talk like a man to avert discovery.

But with a loose-fitting uniform, and with so many boy soldiers barely in their teens, it is not hard to see how a woman could live undetected for months or years. Their identities were often only discovered by accident—for example, one account tells of a woman who was discovered when she fell into a river and had to be rescued—or because of injury or death. A lucky few survived the war without ever being discovered. They served for years alongside their male counterparts and fought in many battles.

Some estimate the number of women who served in the Civil War to be nearly 1,000. Because they passed as men, it is impossible to know the exact number with any certainty.

Passage 8B

According to contemporary accounts, it was well known, both to male soldiers and to ordinary citizens, that women fought in the Union and Confederate armies. Stories by eyewitnesses and even published reports were common. In the case of one woman, Mary Owens, her triumphant return home after a serious injury was widely celebrated in her town and featured in press coverage. She had enlisted in the Union army with her husband, William Evans, and carried on fighting after he had been killed in battle. She served for 18 months under the alias John Evans until treatment for her wounds revealed her gender. Stories of these women were often fodder for gossip in the army camps.

Decades after the war, many families included the details of these women's service in their obituaries. Articles about the soldier-women continued to be written. Unfortunately, the focus, and fascination, of the writers and the reading public appears not to have been with their heroic acts on the field, or with what life was like for them in the camps, but only with the fact that these women had enlisted and whether or not they emerged from the war unscathed.

In addition, the US government maintained information, during and after the war, of the existence of the soldier-women as part of the country's military archives. The US Records and Pension Office kept complete service reports for a number of soldier-women, including discharge papers that list the cause for their expulsion as the fact that their gender was discovered. In later years, some of these women even received a military pension for their service.

Despite such popular recognition, the Union and Confederate armies— and later the US government—officially denied that any woman lived among the rank and file or that any woman had ever fought in the war. And because their stories were told in the general sphere and didn't find their way into school textbooks, the Civil War soldier-women are unknown to most Americans today.

81. The author's primary purpose in writing Passage 8A is to

(A) criticize the small number of women who fought in the Civil War.
(B) expound on the reasons for the lack of women in combat.
(C) bring to light the attitudes of citizens toward Civil War veterans.
(D) describe the history of female soldiers in the Civil War.

82. As used in line 8 of Passage 8A, the word *unconventional* most nearly means

(A) "unusual."
(B) "virulent."
(C) "amateur."
(D) "licentious."

83. With which of the following statements would the author of Passage 8B agree?

I. The Union and Confederate armies were proud that women fought in the Civil War.
II. The existence of soldier-women was no secret during or after the Civil War.
III. Soldier-women of the Civil War accepted Victorian social constraints.

(A) I
(B) II
(C) I and II
(D) II and III

84. The author of Passage 8B mentions Mary Owens in order to

(A) provide evidence of eyewitness accounts and published reports.
(B) imply that the majority of stories about soldier-women are false.
(C) suggest that many eyewitness accounts cannot be trusted.
(D) emphasize the racial inequality of the Union army.

85. As used in line 12 of Passage 8B, the word *fascination* most nearly means

(A) "optimism."
(B) "putrescence."
(C) "interest."
(D) "frailty."

86. The authors of both passages discuss

(A) women who fought in the Union and Confederate armies.
(B) the US Records and Pension Office.
(C) articles and obituaries of Civil War soldier-women.
(D) the US military in the twentieth century.

87. In lines 15–16, the author of Passage 8A suggests reasons why

(A) the Union and Confederate armies prohibited women's enlistment.
(B) so few women were wounded or killed in combat.
(C) the US Records and Pension Office kept complete service reports for soldier-women.
(D) women were able to successfully pass as men in army camps.

88. The attitude of the author of Passage 8A toward women who fought in the Civil War can best be described as

(A) reverent.
(B) onerous.
(C) divisible.
(D) heathenish.

89. In lines 12–14 of Passage 8B, the author implies that

(A) Mary Owens could have remained in service had she not been wounded.
(B) specific details of these women's experiences were often not included in published accounts.
(C) the identities of many soldier-women were only revealed in their obituaries.
(D) the reading public was fascinated by the heroic acts of the soldier-women.

90. As used in line 8 of Passage 8A, the word *embedded* most nearly means

(A) "averted."
(B) "thwarted."
(C) "bewildered."
(D) "rooted."

91. Which of the following statements most accurately describes the relationship between Passage 8A and Passage 8B?

(A) Passage 1 is a direct rebuttal of the ideas in Passage 8B.
(B) Both passages arrive at the same conclusion through different analyses.
(C) The passages address different aspects of the same topic.
(D) Passage 8B provides the evidence to support the conclusions in Passage 8A.

92. Which of the following best describes the "rank and file" mentioned in line 45 of Passage 8B?

(A) The ordinary soldiers of an army, excluding the officers
(B) The tools and armaments of the armies
(C) The clothing and accessories worn by Victorian women
(D) The shackles and chains that held prisoners of war

93. As used in line 15 of Passage 8B, the word *unscathed* most nearly means

(A) "succinct."
(B) "unharmed."
(C) "clement."
(D) "formidable."

CHAPTER 2

Set 2 Critical Reading Questions

Passage 9

From the table at which they had been lunching, two American ladies of ripe but well-cared-for middle age moved across the lofty terrace of the Roman restaurant and, leaning on its parapet, looked first at each other, and then down on the outspread glories of the Palatine and the Forum, with the same expression of vague but benevolent approval.

The luncheon hour was long past, and the two had their end of the vast terrace to themselves. At its opposite extremity, a few groups, detained by a lingering look at the outspread city, were gathering up guidebooks and fumbling for tips. The last of them scattered, and the two ladies were alone on the air-washed height.

"Well, I don't see why we shouldn't just stay here," said Mrs. Slade, the lady of the high color and energetic brows. Two derelict basket chairs stood near, and she pushed them into the angle of the parapet, and settled herself in one, her gaze upon the Palatine. "After all, it's still the most beautiful view in the world."

"It always will be, to me," assented her friend Mrs. Ansley, with so slight a stress on the "me" that Mrs. Slade, though she noticed it, wondered if it were not merely accidental, like the random underlinings of old-fashioned letter writers.

"Grace Ansley was always old fashioned," she thought, and added aloud, with a retrospective smile: "It's a view we've both been familiar with for a good many years. When we first met here, we were younger than our girls are now. You remember!"

"Oh, yes, I remember," murmured Mrs. Ansley, with the same indefinable stress—"There's that headwaiter wondering," she interpolated. She was evidently far less sure of herself and of her rights in the world than Mrs. Slade.

"I'll cure him of wondering," said Mrs. Slade, stretching her hand toward a bag as opulent looking as Mrs. Ansley's. Signing to the headwaiter, she explained that she and her friend were old lovers of Rome and would like to spend the end of the afternoon looking down on the view—that is, if it did not disturb the service! The headwaiter, bowing over her gratuity, assured her that the ladies were most welcome, and would be still more so if they would condescend to remain for dinner. A full-moon night they would remember. . . .

Mrs. Slade's black brows drew together, as though references to the moon were out of place and even unwelcome. But she smiled away her frown as the headwaiter retreated. "Well, why not! We might do worse. There's no knowing, I suppose, when the girls will be back. Do you even know back from where? I don't!"

Mrs. Ansley again colored slightly. "I think those young Italian aviators we met at the embassy invited them to fly to Tarquinia for tea. I suppose they'll want to wait and fly back by moonlight."

"Moonlight—moonlight! What a part it still plays in the lives of young lovers. Do you suppose they're as sentimental as we were?"

"I've come to the conclusion that I don't in the least know what they are," said Mrs. Ansley. "And perhaps we didn't know much more about each other."

"No, perhaps we didn't."

Her friend gave her a shy glance. "I never should have supposed you were sentimental, Alida."

94. In lines 1–2, the narrator uses the phrase "ripe but well-cared-for" to describe

    (A) the restaurant.
    (B) the ladies at lunch.
    (C) the tomato plants.
    (D) the luggage.

95. As used in line 3, the word *parapet* most nearly means

    (A) "nemesis."
    (B) "denouement."
    (C) "zephyr."
    (D) "wall."

96. The narrator's description of the people in lines 7–8 suggests that they are

    (A) pilots.
    (B) tourists.
    (C) actors.
    (D) chauffeurs.

97. It can be inferred from the passage that the scene takes place

    (A) in the late afternoon.
    (B) early in the morning.
    (C) in the middle of the night.
    (D) at dinnertime.

98. As used in line 7, the word *extremity* most nearly means

(A) "bulwark."
(B) "edge."
(C) "limb."
(D) "epitome."

99. Mrs. Slade has "a retrospective smile" because she is

(A) recalling the past.
(B) masking her umbrage.
(C) unhappily married.
(D) cautiously optimistic.

100. In line 28, the narrator uses the phrase "as opulent-looking as Mrs. Ansley's" to suggest that

(A) both ladies are well-to-do women in society.
(B) Mrs. Slade is tagging along with her wealthier friend.
(C) their daughters are very fashionable girls.
(D) Mrs. Slade enjoys traveling with her friend.

101. In the seventh paragraph (lines 27–33), the narrator implies that Mrs. Slade

(A) does not approve of Mrs. Ansley's old-fashioned notions.
(B) addresses the headwaiter condescendingly.
(C) gives the headwaiter some money as a bribe so they can stay there longer.
(D) decided that it would be best for the group that she pay for tomorrow's lunch in advance.

102. In the comparison in lines 25–26, the narrator suggests that

(A) Mrs. Ansley resents Mrs. Slade because Mrs. Slade is a younger woman.
(B) Mrs. Slade would much rather be in Rome without Mrs. Ansley.
(C) Mrs. Ansley doesn't trust the aviators around her daughter.
(D) Mrs. Slade is more gregarious and confident than Mrs. Ansley.

103. In line 26, the narrator suggests that Mrs. Ansley's comment was

(A) never meant to have been heard by Mrs. Slade.
(B) an interruption of Mrs. Slade's recollections of their past together in Rome.
(C) considered by Mrs. Slade to have been extremely rude.
(D) overheard by the tourists at the other end of the terrace.

104. In the last sentence, Mrs. Ansley reveals that she is surprised because

  (A) the last time they had been together in Rome, they fought.
  (B) Mrs. Slade was in deep mourning for her recently deceased husband.
  (C) she did not think Mrs. Slade would be emotional about their youthful adventures.
  (D) the time had passed so quickly since they finished lunch.

105. In the passage, the moonlight is used by the author as a symbol of

  (A) ancient Rome.
  (B) airplanes and navigation.
  (C) changing ocean tides.
  (D) youth and romance.

106. As used in line 47, the word *sentimental* most nearly means

  (A) "maudlin."
  (B) "orthodox."
  (C) "ignoble."
  (D) "nonpareil."

Passage 10

It has been clearly documented that crime levels in the United States have been falling for some time. In fact, crime levels today are at their lowest level since the 1960s. Adding positive news to these statistics is that many states are heeding the call for reforms in sentencing and corrections procedures. The goal of these reforms is not only to keep people out of prison but also to enhance the efficacy of the parole system, for example, by helping to provide adequate housing or employment to convicted felons. Even so, over half of inmates released will be arrested again within three years because of their inability to find a stable job and a place to live, their need for medical care, or a lack of practical education and training.

It is also well known that the jail population of the United States has grown to an alarming size of 2.3 million people in some form of incarceration or detention. Globally, the United States has the highest rate of incarceration at 670 per 100,000 people. Studies have shown that one of the reasons for this dramatic increase is the war on drugs, as a citizen can be arrested for the possession of minute amounts of an illegal substance, and prison sentences for drug offenses are disproportionately long. One in five inmates in federal prison is there for a nonviolent drug offense.

This increase has had the direst consequences in African American communities, where males are six times more likely to be incarcerated than white males. This statistic is also true of black women, whose incarceration rate is four times that of white females. Hispanic and Latino males are two times more likely to be incarcerated than white males. The loss of a central male figure in the household because of incarceration breaks up families and reduces income, raising the poverty level. Children of incarcerated parents are five times more likely to engage in risky or criminal behavior.

There is also an aging prison population in this nation because people are serving more time than those in past decades. More than 160,000 people are serving life sentences, with and without the possibility of parole. Another 44,000 are serving virtual life sentences, where the inmate is not expected to survive to be released. Each year of a prison life sentence that begins in a person's 30s costs an average of $1 million. Seventeen thousand prisoners are serving life sentences for nonviolent crimes.

It is evident that the current measures to substantially reduce the US jail population are a step in the right direction but are not enough. City and state officials must come together to brainstorm new solutions and put forward more reforms to decrease initial incarceration rates and reduce recidivism, lowering the overall prison population over time.

107. Which of the following statements best supports the main point of the passage?

(A) Local communities are often hardest hit by this dire situation.
(B) Reducing incarceration rates will reduce poverty levels and improve the economy.
(C) Most people serving life sentences have the possibility of parole.
(D) There are more people in jail today than there were 20 years ago.

108. As used in line 5, the word *efficacy* most nearly means

(A) "degree."
(B) "competence."
(C) "calumny."
(D) "novice."

109. Based on the second paragraph, the author would most likely agree with which of the following statements:

(A) The United States has more criminals than any other country.
(B) Drug-related crimes are the most serious and deserve the harshest punishments.
(C) The United States has more nonviolent criminals in jail than violent criminals.
(D) Our legal system is more effective at putting criminals in jail.

110. The first paragraph serves mostly to

(A) exculpate the failures of the US judicial system.
(B) explain the current state of US corrections procedures.
(C) provide evidence for the need for the war on drugs.
(D) warn against the consequences of a felony record.

111. In paragraph 2, the word *disproportionately* most nearly means

(A) "equitably."
(B) "logistically."
(C) "unreasonably."
(D) "subtly."

112. In the third paragraph, the author suggests that

(A) the increase of incarceration in America is felt most strongly by minorities.
(B) men are much more likely to be sentenced on drug charges.
(C) women are receiving ineffective or incompetent counsel in the first stages of the criminal justice system.
(D) Hispanics are the second-largest minority group in US prisons.

113. In paragraph 3, the word *direst* most nearly means

(A) "fortuitous."
(B) "quixotic."
(C) "abnormal."
(D) "most severe."

114. The author mentions the aging prison population in order to

(A) emphasize the insidious nature of Alzheimer's disease.
(B) imply that senior citizens are committing more crimes.
(C) provide another reason for the current US jail population crisis.
(D) protest the abolition of the death penalty in most states.

115. In paragraph 4, it could be inferred that the author

(A) does not believe in giving prisoners parole.
(B) believes that many prisoners who have life sentences do not deserve them.
(C) believes the money spent on lifelong prisoners might be better used elsewhere.
(D) does not believe nonviolent offenders should be in jail.

State	Incarcerated Pop. per 100,000	Murder Rate per 100,000	% Pop. below National Poverty Level
Louisiana	1,420	11.8	19.9
Mississippi	1,300	8.0	21.9
Alabama	1,230	8.4	19.2
Minnesota	380	1.8	11.4
Maine	380	1.5	14.0

116. Based on the table, which of the following statements is true?

    (A) States with higher incarceration rates have higher poverty levels.

    (B) States with lower incarceration rates have fewer prisons.

    (C) Murders account for most of the incarcerated population.

    (D) Poor states have more crime.

117. Which of the following statements could be inferred from the table?

    (A) Geographical location has a significant impact on murder rates.

    (B) Southern states have more prisons because the South lost the Civil War.

    (C) Poverty levels are strong indicators of higher crime rates and prison populations.

    (D) The higher incarceration rates are due to more life sentences.

Passage 11

The moon has always held a fascination for civilizations throughout history. It is beautiful and mysterious. It impacts our ocean's tides and feeds superstitions and stories. It also continues to puzzle scientists with no clear answers about its origins.

The moon is thought to have formed more than 4 billion years ago, not long after Earth. There are many theories on how the moon came into existence. One of the earliest theories is the Fission theory that the moon came from the Earth's crust, specifically the Pacific Ocean basin. However, had this been accurate, fossil evidence from the ocean would be consistent with fossil evidence on the moon. No such evidence exists.

Another theory is the Capture theory, in which the moon was created elsewhere in the solar system and was captured into orbit by Earth's gravity. But an event of such perfect timing and force is highly improbable. The Condensation theory, that the moon and Earth were created individually from the same substance that forms the rest of the solar system, was also discarded. The moon lacks an iron core that would have been formed by this genesis.

The most widely accepted explanation is that a low-speed impact occurred between Earth and another object that was likely as big as Mars, which forced tons of material into orbit. All that material then slowly coalesced to form the moon. However, if the moon was created from this type of impact, much of the debris would have come from the other object resulting in a very different chemical composition from Earth. This would also explain the synchronous rotation, meaning the same side of the moon always faces Earth.

However, the far side of the moon may have faced Earth at one time. We know from the age of the craters on the moon's surface that it was hit repeatedly during the creation of the solar system. If the moon had always faced the same way, it would have more craters on one side. The newest theory of the moon's conception holds another possible explanation for this.

"Synestia" is the newest theory that it was a high-speed impact with a Mars-sized object that vaporized some of the outer layers of the Earth, blowing the debris into a ring around the planet. The high speed of the collision increased the rotation speed, and the debris coalesced into an individual body—the moon. Over billions of years, the gravitational pull of the Earth and moon on each other caused the rotations to slow down until they synchronized.

118. The main purpose of the passage is

(A) to explain why the moon has craters.

(B) to compare different theories about the origins of the moon.

(C) to illustrate how the creation of the moon is similar to the creation of the solar system.

(D) to show how ridiculous studying space is because we will never know the true story.

119. Paragraph 1 implies

(A) people have always wondered about the moon.

(B) the moon is pretty but has no significant impact on our lives.

(C) scientists have pretty much figured out everything about the moon.

(D) the moon has always played an important role in civilizations in many ways.

120. In paragraph 3, the word *improbable* most nearly means

(A) "unknown."

(B) "impossible."

(C) "gratuitous."

(D) "questionable."

121. All of the following are reasons the earliest theories of the moon's origin were discarded *except*

(A) there was no fossil evidence showing the moon had once been part of the Pacific Ocean.

(B) condensation has to do with moisture, and there is no water in space.

(C) the timing and force necessary to pull an object from space into Earth's orbit is extremely precise.

(D) the moon does not have an iron core.

122. In paragraph 4, the word *coalesced* most nearly means

(A) "ostracized."

(B) "combined."

(C) "deteriorated."

(D) "interrogated."

123. The author would most likely agree with which of the following statements:

    (A) No one will ever know the true origin of the moon.
    (B) It is important to know how the moon was formed because it may be colonized some day.
    (C) Theories about the moon's origin will probably change as science improves its research abilities.
    (D) How the moon was formed is not very important.

124. In paragraph 4, the word *synchronous* most nearly means

    (A) "opposing."
    (B) "forceful."
    (C) "spinning."
    (D) "simultaneous."

125. In paragraphs 4–6, the author implies

    (A) Earth was once a gas giant like Jupiter or Saturn.
    (B) it is impossible for planets to collide with each other.
    (C) the collision between Earth and the other object was colossal.
    (D) there is still a ton of material in orbit above Earth from that impact.

126. The purpose of the text in paragraph 6 is to

    (A) suggest a possible explanation for the moon's current orientation.
    (B) provide a new hypothesis for the creation of the moon.
    (C) imply the moon is in danger of colliding with another celestial body.
    (D) provide evidence that directly relates to the newest theories of the moon's creation.

127. It can be inferred from the passage that the author believes

    (A) the formation of the moon does not coincide with the formation of the asteroid belt.
    (B) there are several possible causes for there being just one moon orbiting Earth.
    (C) the ages of the craters cannot accurately be determined with today's technology.
    (D) there are aliens living on the far side of the moon.

Passage 12

Factory farming takes an enormous toll on our environment. There are many procedures involved in the large-scale manufacture of food that result in greenhouse gases and other pollutants entering the environment. Some procedures require the consumption of copious amounts of fossil fuels, such as the transportation and refrigeration of food products. The trucks, trains, and planes that carry food around the world are fueled by hundreds of thousands of gallons of gasoline. The electricity required to keep food refrigerated and preserved for human consumption requires the burning of coal or natural gas at power plants. Over 90 million tons of carbon dioxide are released into the atmosphere every year. Although many people are aware of the damaging effects of carbon dioxide, they do not realize that methane, a gas with 25 times more global warming potential than CO_2, accounts for 37 percent of greenhouse gas emissions, making it an ominous concern.

Other factors that detrimentally affect the environment include excessive use of freshwater for irrigation. An increase of pathogens like *E. coli* and salmonella occurs from fresh water sources that have been contaminated by manure and other animal byproducts. Run-off from fossil fuels used in farm equipment, synthetic fertilizers, and pesticides poison these water supplies for drinking and kill off natural food sources and vegetation, impacting natural ecosystems.

The production of beef is more damaging to the environment than that of any other food we consume. Cattle account for 75 percent of farming-related greenhouse gas emissions compared to more environmentally efficient chickens and pigs, which produce only 10 percent of the emissions and provide three times more meat. Grazing is a primary concern. Raising large numbers of cattle requires the production of a vast amount of food for the animals. In North America, livestock consumes the least due to nutrient-rich feed at 165–662 pounds of food per animal annually.

If the cattle are free-range cattle, large areas of land are required for them to live on. In some developing countries, this has led to devastating deforestation and, subsequently, the loss of rare plants and animal species, particularly in tropical rain forests in Central and South America. In the United States, particularly in the Midwest and Rocky Mountains, overgrazing results in soil erosion and increases the danger of flooding and landslides.

Unfortunately, beef consumption is growing rapidly. This is the result of simple supply and demand factors. Specifically, there are two main causes of demand that are spurring the production of more supply. First, the increase in the world population that has taken place since the advent of modern medicine means that there are more people to consume meat. The second factor is socioeconomic advancement. As citizens in developing nations become financially stable, they can afford to buy more meat.

Therefore, the only way to reduce the greenhouse gas emissions is for people around the world to significantly cut down on the amount of beef they eat.

128. The author's primary purpose is to

(A) condemn the practice of deforestation of the rain forest.
(B) explain the effects of the population explosion beginning in the twentieth century.
(C) describe the history of global warming activism.
(D) argue for the reduction of pollution through a decrease in beef production.

129. The conclusion above is flawed because

   (A) governments, companies, and individuals are already doing a lot to reduce the carbon footprint of the beef industry.

   (B) it doesn't take into account other methods of reducing greenhouse gas emissions.

   (C) cutting down on beef consumption would directly increase malnutrition in developed nations.

   (D) raising animals doesn't require the additional, unique considerations that plant production does, such as fertilizer, insecticides, and irrigation.

130. As used in paragraph 1, the word *copious* most nearly means

   (A) "profuse."

   (B) "dubious."

   (C) "amicable."

   (D) "impeccable."

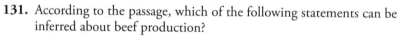

131. According to the passage, which of the following statements can be inferred about beef production?

   I. The practice of raising free-range cattle is friendlier to the environment than traditional methods.

   II. Beef production generates a lot of greenhouse gases because the cattle release large amounts of methane.

   III. The money to be made by raising cattle is a motivating factor in cutting down otherwise unprofitable rain forests.

   (A) I

   (B) II

   (C) I and II

   (D) II and III

132. The author would most likely agree with which of the following statements?

   (A) Beef production generates more greenhouse gases than production of any other food we consume.

   (B) Developing nations consume too much of the world's beef.

   (C) Food production is a more dire concern than global warming.

   (D) Global warming is the direct result of advances in modern medicine.

133. As used in paragraph 2, the word *detrimentally* most nearly means

   (A) "obsequiously."

   (B) "destructively."

   (C) "informatively."

   (D) "cooperatively."

134. The purpose of paragraph 4 is

(A) to convince farmers to raise pigs and chickens instead of cattle.

(B) to give examples of the mistreatment of cattle.

(C) to provide evidence of how cattle farming impacts the lands.

(D) to explain how feeding cattle costs a lot of money.

135. As used paragraph 1, the word *ominous* most nearly means

(A) "mundane."

(B) "dire."

(C) "garrulous."

(D) "deliberate."

136. The primary purpose of the fifth paragraph is to

(A) emphasize the socioeconomic advantages of beef production.

(B) explain the growing scale of the beef production industry.

(C) delineate the global warming issues that plague our society.

(D) illustrate the effect of modern medicine on the beef industry.

137. As used in paragraph 4, the word *subsequently* most nearly means

(A) "beforehand."

(B) "simultaneously."

(C) "afterward."

(D) "exclusively."

138. In paragraph 2, the main idea is that

(A) people are getting sick from salmonella because they don't wash their food.

(B) farms are using too much water for irrigation and not providing enough drinking water to cattle.

(C) farming results in contaminated water that can affect entire ecosystems.

(D) farms should be responsible for treating contaminated water to reuse it.

139. According to the passage, methane is a serious environmental concern because

(A) the cattle can become sick from overabundant emissions.

(B) its potential effect on the environment is many times greater than that of carbon dioxide.

(C) most people are unaware of the existence of methane as part of the atmosphere.

(D) it forms a toxic gas when it is combined with carbon dioxide.

140. As used in paragraph 5, the word *spurring* most nearly means

(A) "insulting."
(B) "restricting."
(C) "motivating."
(D) "enhancing."

Passage 13A

The assemblage of Egyptian antiquities in the British Museum in London is the world's largest and most comprehensive outside of Egypt. Founded in 1753, the original collections were comprised mostly of artifacts bequeathed to the museum by Sir Hans Sloane upon his death. By 1866, the museum housed approximately 10,000 objects.

One of the greatest periods of expansion for the collections took place in the early nineteenth century. Napoleon's forces had invaded the region, intending to make it a stepping-stone in the conquest of British India. However, the French forces were defeated in the Battle of the Nile. All of the Egyptian antiquities that had been acquired by the French were commandeered by the British army and offered to the British Museum as part of the treaty in 1803. Among the many works taken at that time was the legendary Rosetta Stone, which made possible our modern understanding of Egyptian hieroglyphs.

Subsequently, the British Museum actively supported excavations in Egypt into the twentieth century. By 1924, the collection contained more than 50,000 objects. The museum gained hundreds more acquisitions until changes were made to antiquities laws in Egypt. In the 2000s alone, millions of items were given to the British Museum's Egyptian collections by benefactors from around the world.

Some nations protest that so many cultural artifacts are housed outside of Egypt's borders. Currently, many countries around the world are trying to repatriate objects to their original homelands. A concerted effort is being made to reduce illegal acquisition of cultural artifacts. However, the fact remains that many of these objects would have been lost or destroyed hundreds of years ago had they not been placed in the British Museum's collection. The relics of the past belong to humanity, not just to nation-states, and they should be shared by all, and for all.

Passage 13B

As shocking as it may seem, the shameful ownership of ill-gotten antiquities has continued unabated around the world for much of recent history, despite a number of laws and international agreements that came into force in the last century to work toward ending the trafficking of illegally possessed artifacts and art around the world. As early as the turn of the twentieth century, nations around the world began to make it official government policy that all cultural property belongs to the country, not to an excavator or buyer.

The practice of cultural racketeering is especially high in countries that are suffering from economic crisis. For example, Egypt, Libya, Syria, Peru, and Guatemala are some of the countries severely impacted by the loss of national treasures and historical artifacts. The losses are not only financial but also affect the nation's cultural identity and unity. Stolen artifacts are often resold on the black market to private collectors or to fund other illegal activities.

At present, the United Nations Educational, Scientific and Cultural Organization (UNESCO) 1970 Convention on the Means of Prohibiting the Illicit Import, Export and Transfer of Ownership of Cultural Property is the world's most influential and vigorous international antiquities agreement. The nations that signed the agreement and became members of the convention are allowed to repossess stolen or illegally exported antiquities from other member states. Sadly, not all nations joined the convention immediately. For example, the United States did not incorporate the agreement into American law until 1983, and Britain did not become a signatory nation until 2001.

Although it is important for nations of the world to carefully preserve and share their cultural history with other nations—and institutions such as museums, auction houses, and art galleries have been essential tools in that endeavor—each nation that has had antiquities pilfered from them for centuries should have the right to reclaim those items. However, galleries and museums do not want to give up items that may have cost millions of dollars to attain. The only solution is to share the artifacts through traveling exhibitions, with the explicit understanding that they are simply on loan.

141. The authors of both passages describe

    (A) the acquisition of antiquities.
    (B) the UNESCO convention.
    (C) the British Museum.
    (D) the Battle of the Nile.

142. As used in paragraph 1 of Passage 13A, the word *bequeathed* most nearly means

    (A) "seized."
    (B) "donated."
    (C) "acquired."
    (D) "accessorized."

143. It can be inferred from lines 16–17 of Passage 13A that

    (A) the British Museum has given away more than 12 million items in the 2000s alone.
    (B) the Egyptian government is the new benefactor of the British Museum.
    (C) millions of objects have also been donated to the museum's Egyptian collections.
    (D) the British Museum's collection today contains 50,000 objects.

144. Which of the following statements best describes the changes mentioned in lines 14–15 of Passage 13A?

(A) The British Museum actively supported excavations in the twentieth century.

(B) Antiquities laws in Egypt were modified to prohibit foreigners from funding and conducting excavations.

(C) The UNESCO convention is the world's most influential and vigorous international antiquities agreement.

(D) The Rosetta Stone is the most important ancient artifact ever found.

145. The author's primary purpose in writing Passage 13B is to

(A) recommend new amendments to the UNESCO convention.

(B) explain the lack of Egyptian antiquities in the United States.

(C) criticize the continued ownership of stolen antiquities.

(D) emphasize the benefits of museum collections.

146. According to Passage 13A, which of the following statements is *not* true about the British Museum?

(A) The museum's Egyptian collections have been sequestered by the Egyptian government.

(B) The museum has held the Rosetta Stone since 1803.

(C) The museum has more than 12 million objects in its Egyptian collections.

(D) The museum was founded in 1753.

147. Which of the following statements is *not* supported by the third paragraph of Passage 13B?

(A) It took years for a number of nations to finally become members of the UNESCO convention.

(B) The UNESCO convention became US law through the Convention on Cultural Property Implementation Act.

(C) UNESCO members can recuperate antiquities from other member states.

(D) The UNESCO convention is a robust international agreement regarding antiquities.

148. Which of the following statements most accurately describes the relationship between Passage 13A and Passage 13B?

(A) Passage 13A is a direct rebuttal of the ideas in Passage 13B.

(B) Both passages arrive at the same conclusion through different analyses.

(C) Passage 13A provides an alternative theory to that of Passage 13B.

(D) The passages discuss the same topics, but they focus on different aspects of the topics.

149. As used in paragraph 4 in Passage 13A, the word *repatriate* most nearly means

(A) "patriotic."
(B) "authenticate."
(C) "retaliate."
(D) "export."

150. Which one of the following statements can be inferred from Passage 13A?

(A) Changes in Egyptian antiquities laws meant that finds from excavations were legalized.
(B) The antiquities laws in Egypt were updated after a long, drawn-out battle between the national government of Egypt and collectors in foreign countries.
(C) The Rosetta Stone was the most important Egyptian artifact ever recovered.
(D) The Egyptian galleries can display only a minuscule percentage of the British Museum's Egyptian holdings.

151. As used in paragraph 1 of Passage 13B, the word *unabated* most nearly means

(A) "unsubstantiated."
(B) "subsided."
(C) "unhindered."
(D) "contaminated."

152. As used in line 26 of Passage 13B, the word *pilfered* most nearly means

(A) "berated,"
(B) "curtailed."
(C) "stolen."
(D) "refuted."

153. Paragraph 2 of Passage 13B implies

(A) that only poor countries are victims of artifact thefts.
(B) countries in crisis should sell their artifacts to help raise money for their people.
(C) the loss of national cultural and historical treasures affects countries in multiple ways.
(D) if countries cannot protect their treasures, they deserve to lose them.

Passage 14

Excerpt from "The Yellow Wallpaper" by Charlotte Perkins Gilman

If a physician of high standing, and one's own husband, assures friends and relatives that there is really nothing the matter with one but temporary nervous depression—a slight hysterical tendency—what is one to do?

My brother is also a physician and also of high standing, and he says the same thing.

So I take phosphates or phosphites—whichever it is—and tonics and journeys and air and exercise, and am absolutely forbidden to "work" until I am well again.

Personally, I disagree with their ideas.

Personally, I believe that congenial work, with excitement and change, would do me good.

But what is one to do?

I did write for a while in spite of them; but it *does* exhaust me a good deal—having to be so sly about it, or else meet with heavy opposition.

I sometimes fancy that in my condition if I had less opposition and more society and stimulus—but John says the very worst thing I can do is to think about my condition, and I confess it always makes me feel bad.

So I will let it alone and talk about the house.

The most beautiful place! It is quite alone, standing well back from the road, quite three miles from the village. It makes me think of English places that you read about, for there are hedges and walls and gates that lock, and lots of separate little houses for the gardeners and people.

There is a *delicious* garden! I never saw such a garden—large and shady, full of box-bordered paths, and lined with long grape-covered arbors with seats under them.

There were greenhouses too, but they are all broken now.

There was some legal trouble, I believe, something about the heirs and coheirs; anyhow, the place has been empty for years.

That spoils my ghostliness, I am afraid, but I don't care—there is something strange about the house—I can feel it.

I even said so to John one moonlight evening, but he said what I felt was a *draught*, and shut the window.

I get unreasonably angry with John sometimes. I'm sure I never used to be so sensitive. I think it is due to this nervous condition.

But John says if I feel so, I shall neglect proper self-control; so I take pains to control myself—before him, at least, and that makes me very tired.

I don't like our room a bit. I wanted one downstairs that opened on the piazza and had roses all over the window, and such pretty old-fashioned chintz hangings! But John would not hear of it.

He said there was only one window and not room for two beds, and no near room for him if he took another.

He is very careful and loving, and hardly lets me stir without special direction.

I have a schedule prescription for each hour in the day; he takes all care from me, and so I feel basely ungrateful not to value it more.

He said we came here solely on my account, that I was to have perfect rest and all the air I could get. "Your exercise depends on your strength, my dear," said he, "and your food somewhat on your appetite; but air you can absorb all the time." So we took the nursery at the top of the house.

It is a big, airy room, the whole floor nearly, with windows that look all ways, and air and sunshine galore. It was nursery first and then playroom and gymnasium, I should judge; for the windows are barred for little children, and there are rings and things in the walls.

The paint and paper look as if a boys' school had used it. It is stripped off—the paper—in great patches all around the head of my bed, about as far as I can reach, and in a great place on the other side of the room low down. I never saw a worse paper in my life.

One of those sprawling flamboyant patterns committing every artistic sin.

It is dull enough to confuse the eye in following, pronounced enough to constantly irritate and provoke study, and when you follow the lame uncertain curves for a little distance they suddenly commit suicide—plunge off at outrageous angles, destroy themselves in unheard of contradictions.

The color is repellent, almost revolting; a smoldering unclean yellow, strangely faded by the slow-turning sunlight.

It is a dull yet lurid orange in some places, a sickly sulfur tint in others.

No wonder the children hated it! I should hate it myself if I had to live in this room long.

There comes John, and I must put this away—he hates to have me write a word.

154. The passage is written in which point of view?

(A) First person
(B) Second person
(C) Third-person limited
(D) Third-person omniscient

155. The treatments for the speaker's condition involve all of the following *except*

(A) fresh air.
(B) exercise.
(C) tonics.
(D) isolation.

156. The repetition of the word *personally* implies

    (A) the speaker has a high opinion of herself.

    (B) she feels her husband is overprotective.

    (C) she is amused by her husband's and brother's opinions.

    (D) she truly does have a nervous disorder.

157. The word *draught* most nearly means

    (A) "a tonic."

    (B) "a draft."

    (C) "chills."

    (D) "a premonition."

158. The narrator's tone when describing the house can be best characterized as

    (A) critical and snobby.

    (B) objective and detached.

    (C) romantic and whimsical.

    (D) depressed and fearful.

159. The speaker most desires to spend her time

    (A) writing.

    (B) following her dreams.

    (C) spending time with friends.

    (D) escaping her husband.

160. The word *flamboyant* most nearly means

    (A) "gaudy,"

    (B) "artsy."

    (C) "calming."

    (D) "bland."

161. The speaker's husband is best described as

    (A) controlling and pragmatic.

    (B) loving and thoughtful.

    (C) skilled and sarcastic.

    (D) punctilious and harsh.

162. The narrator's attitude toward her husband's treatment of her might best be described as

    (A) defiant.

    (B) resigned.

    (C) loving.

    (D) frustrated.

163. The speaker's "slight hysterical tendencies" are most clearly demonstrated by her

(A) fixation upon the strange nature of the house.
(B) desire to have a room with chintz hangings.
(C) secretive writing.
(D) obsession with the wallpaper in her room.

164. What is one major similarity between the narrator's room and the wallpaper's pattern?

(A) They both are chaotic.
(B) They both do not let in sunshine.
(C) They both have windows.
(D) They both have bars.

165. "The Yellow Wallpaper" is written in the style of a

(A) dialogue between the narrator and her husband.
(B) stream of consciousness.
(C) series of notes.
(D) flashback.

Passage 15

With the world's population swelling and the water supply dwindling, the availability of freshwater for human consumption is a growing concern. One-sixth of the world's population does not have access to clean drinking water. Two million people die each year from a lack of clean, freshwater for drinking, cooking, and everyday needs. Agriculture and industry account for 90 percent of freshwater use around the world.

Aquifers are a main source of freshwater. Rainwater seeps into the ground through porous rock where it is stored until a well is drilled for access. However, the lakes, rivers, and streams that feed these aquifers are drying up due to a lack of rain and meltwater running off mountains. The Colorado River has dried up so much it no longer runs all the way to the ocean. California's aquifers are diminishing up to 11 inches a year.

Water consumption is expected to grow 55 percent by the year 2050. However, freshwater continues to be compromised by poor distribution management, overdevelopment, bacteria, and diseases, in addition to the effects of climate change.

As sources of water disappear, methods for producing freshwater are being explored on a large scale. Desalination of ocean water is growing in popularity. However, it is a costly process and there are concerns that the energy needed to run these plants creates even more pollution. Some countries are experimenting with solar-powered desalination technologies. Another option is treating wastewater to be reused.

Steps have also been taken to encourage developed nations to use water more economically. Manufacturers now produce toilets that need almost no water to remove waste, as well as appliances that are much more efficient. Public awareness campaigns are also common, urging people to use less water during their daily routine, such as when they shower or brush their teeth. Using sprinkler systems on timers to water gardens and lawns saves hundreds of gallons of water per year. Solar panels reduce the need to produce electricity with fossil fuels that contaminate water sources. The government offers tax breaks and bonuses for purchasing other energy saving items for homes. While these steps are laudable, more needs to be done to protect the water sources that remain and share the water responsibly between all countries.

166. As used in paragraph 2, the word *dwindling* most nearly means

(A) "insatiable."
(B) "decreasing."
(C) "deleterious."
(D) "sedentary."

167. Which of the following statements support(s) the main point of the passage?

  I. Fresh water is being used up faster than it is being replaced.
  II. There are many methods of reducing excessive water use.
  III. Desalination is the process of removing excess salt and other minerals from water.

(A) I
(B) II
(C) II and III
(D) I and II

168. The main purpose of paragraph 2 is to

(A) blame California for the freshwater crisis in America.
(B) describe all the freshwater sources located in Colorado.
(C) explain what an aquifer is and how it is impacted by shrinking water resources.
(D) support drilling wells instead of using water from lakes and streams.

169. Which of the following is *not* mentioned as a possible cause of decreased availability of freshwater?

(A) A smaller number of freshwater sources
(B) The harmful effects of desalination to the environment
(C) Wasteful use of freshwater in developed nations
(D) The cost of establishing new freshwater projects

170. As used in paragraph 2, the word *porous* most nearly means

- (A) "saturated."
- (B) "absorbent."
- (C) "resilient."
- (D) "dense."

171. Paragraph 4 suggests that the author believes that

- (A) desalination is a problematic and unwise solution.
- (B) dishwashers should be made much more efficient.
- (C) efforts are being made to find cost effective solutions for freshwater production.
- (D) public awareness campaigns have been ineffective.

172. In paragraph 2 the word *consumption* most nearly means

- (A) "ingestion."
- (B) "digestion."
- (C) "purification."
- (D) "evaporation."

173. All of the following are strategies to improve water efficiency *except*

- (A) manufacturing low-flow toilets.
- (B) installing solar panels on your house.
- (C) leaving the water on cold when you wash dishes or brush your teeth.
- (D) using irrigation systems to water lawns and gardens instead of running a hose.

174. The author would most likely agree with which of the following statements?

- (A) People should drink less water to conserve our remaining resources.
- (B) The water crisis needs to be addressed on a global scale.
- (C) If we stop pollution, the water will return to its previous amounts.
- (D) No matter what we do, the world is going to run out of freshwater.

175. The main purpose of this passage is

- (A) to show how governments are wasting the world's freshwater.
- (B) to criticize people for being wasteful with water.
- (C) to look at the dangers, causes, and potential solutions to the freshwater crisis.
- (D) to scare people into changing their water usage habits.

176. In paragraph 4, all of the following words are synonyms for *laudable except*

(A) *commendable.*

(B) *admirable.*

(C) *ineffectual.*

(D) *praiseworthy.*

177. The tone of the passage is

(A) excited.

(B) pessimistic.

(C) condemning.

(D) urgent.

Passage 16

Excerpt from speech given on the opening of the Brooklyn Bridge by Abram S. Hewitt

In no previous period of the world's history could this bridge have been built. Within the last hundred years, the greater part of the knowledge necessary for its erection has been gained. Chemistry was not born until 1776, the year when political economy was ushered into the world by Adam Smith, and the Declaration of Independence was proclaimed by the Continental Congress, to be maintained at the point of the sword by George Washington. In the same year Watt produced his successful steam engine, and a century has not elapsed since the first specimen of his skill was erected on this continent. The law of gravitation was indeed known a hundred years ago, but the intricate laws of force, which now control the domain of industry, had not been developed by the study of physical science, and their practical applications have only been effectually accomplished within our own day, and indeed, some of the most important of them during the building of the bridge. For use in the caissons, the perfecting of the electric light came too late, though happily in season for the illumination of the finished work.

This construction has not only employed every abstract conclusion and formula of mathematics, whether derived from the study of the earth or the heavens, but the whole structure may be said to rest upon a mathematical foundation. The great discoveries of chemistry, showing the composition of water, the nature of gases, the properties of metals; the laws and processes of physics, from the strains and pressures of mighty masses, to the delicate vibrations of molecules, are all recorded here. Every department of human industry is represented, from the quarrying and the cutting of the stones, the mining and smelting of the ores, the conversion of iron into steel by the pneumatic process, to the final shaping of the masses of metal into useful forms, and its reduction into wire, so as to develop in the highest degree, the tensile strength which fits it for the work of suspension. Every tool that the ingenuity of man has invented, has somewhere, in some special detail, contributed its share in the accomplishment of the final result.

"Ah! what a wondrous thing it is to note how many wheels of toil one word, one thought can set in motion."

But without the most recent discoveries of science, which have enabled steel to be substituted for iron—applications made since the original plans of the bridge were devised—we should have had a structure fit, indeed, for use, but of such moderate capacity that we could not have justified the claim which we are now able to make, that the cities of New York and Brooklyn have constructed, and today rejoice in the possession of, the crowning glory of an age memorable for great industrial achievements.

But the bridge is more than an embodiment of the scientific knowledge of physical laws, or a symbol of social tendencies. It is equally a monument to the moral qualities of the human soul. It could never have been built by mere knowledge and scientific skill alone. It required, in addition, the infinite patience and unwearied courage by which great results are achieved. It demanded the endurance of heat, and cold, and physical distress. Its constructors have had to face death in its most repulsive form. Death, indeed, was the fate of its great projector, and dread disease the heritage of the greater engineer, who has brought it to completion. The faith of the saint and the courage of the hero have been combined in the conception, the design, and the execution of this work.

178. The main purpose of the passage is
  (A) to describe the purpose of building the Brooklyn Bridge.
  (B) to pay tribute to the architect who designed the bridge.
  (C) to explain why the bridge was so expensive.
  (D) to honor all of the various areas of knowledge and skills that went into designing and building the bridge.

179. Paragraph 1 implies that
  (A) science was not advanced enough to build this bridge until now.
  (B) no one wanted to try to build the bridge and fail.
  (C) the bridge had to defy gravity.
  (D) they had to wait for electricity to be invented before building the bridge.

180. In paragraph 1, "intricate laws of force" refers to
  (A) chemistry.
  (B) gravity.
  (C) physics.
  (D) biology.

181. In paragraph 1, the word *effectually* most likely means

(A) "effectively."
(B) "effortlessly."
(C) "elaborately."
(D) "eventually."

182. The main purpose of paragraph 2 is to

(A) show off how smart the speaker is.
(B) express gratitude toward the workers who made the bridge possible through their expertise.
(C) illustrate how much skill and information was required to build this bridge.
(D) impress people with the complexity of the building process.

183. In paragraph 2, the word *ingenuity* most nearly means

(A) "motivation."
(B) "sincerity."
(C) "knowledge."
(D) "creativity."

184. The overall tone of the passage is

(A) persuasive and supportive.
(B) grandiose and flamboyant.
(C) provoking and irritable.
(D) complicated and condescending.

185. In the following quote, "Ah! what a wondrous thing it is to note how many wheels of toil one word, one thought can set in motion," the phrase "wheels of toil" is an example of

(A) simile.
(B) metaphor.
(C) hyperbole.
(D) personification.

186. The speaker would most likely agree with all of the following statements *except* that

(A) the Brooklyn Bridge is one of the greatest accomplishments in the history of New York.
(B) the Brooklyn Bridge represents the collaboration of all types of human industry and skills.
(C) the Brooklyn Bridge was still not big enough to accommodate all the traffic that would use it in the future.
(D) the Brooklyn Bridge symbolizes the patience, creativity, and courage of the people who designed and built it.

187. In paragraph 5, it can be inferred that "the moral qualities of the human soul" are

   I. patience.
   II. courage.
   III. scientific knowledge.
   IV. endurance.
   (A) I
   (B) I and III
   (C) II, III, and IV
   (D) I, II, and IV

188. In paragraph 5, the word *execution* most likely means

   (A) the end of the project.
   (B) the death of the architect.
   (C) the implementation of the plan.
   (D) the expenses incurred.

CHAPTER 3

Set 3 Critical Reading Questions

Passage 17

The current energy crisis over crude oil threatens the political and social stability of all countries, regardless of their economic development. Ever-increasing demand—coal, oil, and natural gas (fossil fuels) account for 80 percent of the world's current energy—will eventually outstrip global supply. Estimates of how much crude oil there is vary, but some believe, at the current global consumption rate, that there are only 30 years of resources left. As supplies diminish, this will lead to conflict, and possibly even war, between the nations that supply the crude oil and those that require the product.

Crude oil is crucial to daily life, but few nations today have access to large, easily recoverable deposits. This creates increased political tensions between nation-states. Four regions—Africa, Russia, the Caspian Basin, and the Persian Gulf—account for 80 percent of the world's oil supply, and over half the world's natural gas reserves are in only three countries: Russia, Iran, and Qatar. All of these regions struggle with political instability and tense relationships with other nations in the world. Therefore, in order to avoid dependence on hostile nations, the oil and gas industries in countries like Canada and the United States have turned to unconventional methods of extracting crude oil from less accessible areas, such as tar sands and shale rock deposits.

These methods, while necessary, are nascent and controversial. For example, some experts believe that more studies need to be done on the effects of the hydrofracking process to remove oil and natural gas from shale rock by drilling tunnels and injecting high pressure mixtures into the ground to force the gas out. The effects of using this method are controversial as recent studies show that it might cause earthquakes and pollute local water supplies. In some cases, unconventional methods of oil and gas extraction are prohibitively expensive.

As a result of these issues, many national governments and major oil companies are working on developing other sources of energy, such as solar panels, wind farms, hydroelectric plants, and fuel from corn. However, many of these methods are still in their infancy. The technology has not evolved to the point where the energy derived is dependable. For example, low rainfall means that the output from hydroelectric plants drops precipitously. Power utilities still need plants that run on fossil fuels to make up the shortfall. Another renewable option is nuclear power. Although it has been in use by some countries for several decades, many nations feel that the risks are too great. A nuclear meltdown would be unpredictable, deadly, and catastrophic—be it caused by a natural disaster or human failure.

Additionally, the energy crisis serves to further marginalize the poor, who will find themselves priced out of transportation options, and maybe even food. As the standard of living improves in countries like India, Indonesia, China, and Brazil, more people move to big cities, where the jobs are, or they travel there from their homes in nearby towns. With more employment, they are then able to save money to purchase automobiles and the gasoline to fuel them. However, high-priced gasoline means that they lose access to the educational and job opportunities that were previously available to them. The few public transportation options that exist are poorly maintained, further inhibiting their progress. Even in developed nations, costly gasoline has a profoundly detrimental effect on underprivileged communities.

Food availability will be a problem because logistics and manufacturing are predominantly dependent on crude oil. The food that is grown or produced must be transported from its point of origin out to markets around the world. The more expensive gasoline is, the more costly the food will be, because producers will need to increase the price of the final product in order to cover their cost of operations. Even staples like bread, milk, and rice will become more expensive, threatening the ability of the world's poor to put food on the table.

For now, the world economy depends on the production and dissemination of crude oil. Therefore, with global demand for oil accelerating, the best way to avoid dangerous conflicts is to get more fuel-efficient cars on the roads, reduce our dependence on driving by offering incentives for walking and bicycling, and build more effective public transportation systems.

189. Based on the passage, the author would most likely describe the current energy crisis as

(A)   the cause of underfunded hydrofracking studies.
(B)   a dangerous and urgent threat to global peace and economic stability.
(C)   a consequence of ambitious automobile marketing campaigns.
(E)   the impetus for research into sources of water pollution.

190. As used in paragraph 3, the word *prohibitively* most likely means

(A)   "cheaply."
(B)   "zealously."
(C)   "exorbitantly."
(D)   "perniciously."

191. In the third paragraph, the author suggests that

(A) unconventional methods of extracting crude oil are financially improbable.

(B) tar sands or shale rock deposits are found only in North America.

(C) political tensions are shaping the progress of the oil industry.

(D) easily recoverable deposits can be found all over the world.

192. Which of the following statements best describes the "problem" mentioned in the sixth paragraph?

(A) The production of crude oil is dependent on logistics and food availability.

(B) The high cost of gasoline means the poor lose access to educational and job opportunities.

(C) The cost of operations for food producers depends on the ability of workers to find adequate transportation options.

(D) Producers will raise prices, which means the poor will be unable to purchase sufficient amounts of even the most basic food products.

193. As used in paragraph 3, the word *precipitously* most nearly means

(A) "scurrilously."

(B) "demurely."

(C) "vacuously."

(D) "sharply."

194. Which of the following most accurately describes the purpose of the fourth paragraph?

(A) To highlight the effect of low rainfall on the environment

(B) To describe the problems surrounding the development of alternative sources of energy

(C) To explain how renewable sources currently have the largest share of the energy market

(D) To illustrate the harmful effects of the hydrofracking process

195. As used in paragraph 5, the word *marginalized* most nearly means

(A) "relegated."

(B) "condemned."

(C) "enabled."

(D) "erased."

196. Which of the following statements is *not* supported by the passage?

(A) The energy derived from renewable sources is not dependable.

(B) The crude-oil supply quandary threatens the political and social stability of all countries.

(C) More public transportation options need to be available around the world.

(D) Hydrofracking allows for the extraction of infinite deposits of crude oil.

197. As used in the final paragraph, the word *dissemination* most nearly means

(A) "juxtaposition."
(B) "suspension."
(C) "locomotion."
(D) "distribution."

198. Paragraph 3 suggests that the author regards unconventional methods of extracting crude oil as

(A) new technologies that are essential, but experimental and divisive.
(B) the only method available to meet the considerable current global demand for energy.
(C) incompatible with other sources of energy, such as wind or solar power.
(D) available only in areas that have renewable energy options as well.

199. Which of the following statements would reconcile the discrepancy in the last paragraph?

(A) The current energy crisis will most likely worsen before it gets better.
(B) Other forms of energy consumption, such as electricity for homes and businesses, are not a significant factor in the current energy crisis.
(C) Governments around the world have not enacted any laws or policies to curb dependence on individual car ownership.
(D) Higher prices at the gas pump would go much further in convincing people to drive less.

200. The reason why some nations do not use nuclear power is that

(A) the cost of running nuclear power plants is too high.
(B) there is no longer a need for nuclear energy.
(C) the effect of a plant meltdown would be too devastating.
(D) the energy produced is too short-lived.

Passage 18

The relentless growth of the internet continues to produce phenomena— from email and instant messaging to social networking and real-time communications—that are transforming society. The increasingly significant field of Web science aims to discover and analyze how websites, trends, and virtual interactions and transactions occur and how they impact society positively or negatively. It involves observation of the micro interactions of people on the Web, such as instant-messaging conversations, as well as the macro effects of the internet on the world stage, such as YouTube stardom. The benefits and dangers of internet use often depend on who is using it and how.

For example, Facebook currently has over a billion and a half profiles globally. Families and friends, hundreds or thousands of miles apart, can share news and stay connected instantly. Businesses can reach out to and interact with customers on a more personal level. Communities can increase publicity and attendance to their events, and awareness movements can spread rapidly throughout regions, states, and even countries. But even Facebook has a darker side.

Cyberbullying is rampant through social media. Over 43 percent of children have experienced some form of cyberbullying through harassment, threats, ridicule, and intimidation. This can result in low self-esteem, fear, depression, and even suicide. Facebook and other social media sites should have intense monitoring of content to prevent posts from inciting violence, hate speech, and other illegal activity.

Another serious problem the internet faces is cyberstalking. Cyberstalking is using email, social media, technology, and websites to stalk, follow, or obsess over a person. Sometimes it is a person from a former relationship or a mentally ill person who is delusional and believes this person is a friend. Identity theft is the most serious form of cyberstalking.

Identity theft involves a criminal who steals the identity of a person, usually through personal information the person has shared on the internet. The criminal can then steal money, open new bank accounts, forge documents, and cause havoc in the victim's life.

Preventing and stopping cybercrime is very difficult. There is usually very little evidence, and sometimes a person does not know he or she is a victim. Web science studies are showing that the best way to prevent problems is to make Web pages and Web interactions more trustworthy.

Best practices based on recent findings include visiting pages created by sources such as universities, as well as those that encourage the use of reputable services such as PayPal. Using internet security programs to protect yourself and your computer can help against spyware, viruses, and hacking. Don't share passwords, and keep social media settings as private as possible. No one is 100 percent protected, but a few simple steps can protect people from most cybercrimes, and reporting any suspicious activity can help save other possible victims.

201. Which of the following statements best supports the main point?

(A) Social norms have the greatest impact on the Web.

(B) The internet is too dangerous to use for any personal transactions, and people should go back to using traditional shopping methods.

(C) The internet has positive and negative aspects that should be considered carefully when using it.

(D) The Web was created as a tool for researchers and is the best place to find information.

202. The main purpose of paragraph 1 is

(A) to describe the growth of internet use over time.
(B) to explain the field of Web science.
(C) to warn of the dangers of using the internet.
(D) to illustrate how people are being spied on by scientists.

203. All of the following statements are benefits of using social media *except*

(A) staying connected to friends and families.
(B) having more interaction with customers.
(C) increasing public awareness of events.
(D) sharing private videos and photos with strangers.

204. In paragraph 3, the word *rampant* most likely means

(A) "vicious."
(B) "ubiquitous."
(C) "contagious."
(D) "exclusive."

205. The author would most likely agree with which of the following statements about paragraph 3?

(A) Facebook is at fault for allowing cyberbullying to occur.
(B) Children who are cyberbullied should stay off social media if it makes them feel bad.
(C) Social media companies should monitor their sites more closely for cyberbullying and take a stand against it.
(D) Parents should sue social media sites if their children are victims of cyberbullying, to teach the people who are cyberbullies a lesson.

206. In paragraph 3, the word *inciting* most nearly means

(A) "disseminating."
(B) "condemning."
(C) "provoking."
(D) "celebrating."

207. All of the following statements are reasons cybercrime is difficult to prevent *except*

(A) there is very little evidence a crime occurred.
(B) a person might not recognize being a victim.
(C) it is easy to tamper with computer evidence.
(D) people do not take the right security precautions.

208. Someone who commits identity theft might

(A) try to move into the victim's house.
(B) open credit cards in the victim's name.
(C) steal another person's job.
(D) fake his or her own death.

209. In paragraph 4, the word *havoc* most likely means

(A) "chaos."
(B) "attrition."
(C) "vengeance."
(D) "remorse."

**Number of online conversations
reporting bullying or being bullied**

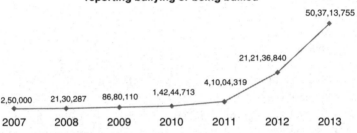

50,37,13,755

21,21,36,840

4,10,04,319

2,50,000   21,30,287   86,80,110   1,42,44,713

2007   2008   2009   2010   2011   2012   2013

—◆— Number of online conversations reporting bullying or being bullied

210. According to the graph, which of the following statements is most likely true?

(A) Cyberbullying has increased 2000 percent in less than a decade.
(B) Bullying only became a serious problem when people started using social media.
(C) The graph is not useful because it doesn't specify which social media site is being used.
(D) Bullying is the most widespread cybercrime happening in 2013.

211. The graph implies

  I. more instances of cyberbullying are being reported.
 II. people are bigger bullies in 2013 than in 2007.
III. advancing technology makes bullying easier.

(A) I
(B) I and II
(C) II and III
(D) I and III

212. We can infer from the conclusion that

(A) cybercrime cannot be stopped.

(B) cyberbullying is the most serious cybercrime.

(C) people can take actions to protect themselves from cybercrime.

(D) it is the responsibility of social media sites to protect users.

Passage 19

Excerpt from "Rappacini's Daughter" by Nathaniel Hawthorne

Nothing could exceed the intentness with which this scientific gardener examined every shrub which grew in his path; it seemed as if he was looking into their inmost nature, making observations in regard to their creative essence, and discovering why one leaf grew in this shape, and another in that, and wherefore such and such flowers differed among themselves in hue and perfume. Nevertheless, in spite of the deep intelligence on his part, there was no approach to intimacy between himself and these vegetable existences. On the contrary, he avoided their actual touch, or the direct inhaling of their odors, with a caution that impressed Giovanni most disagreeably; for the man's demeanor was that of one walking among malignant influences, such as savage beasts, or deadly snakes, or evil spirits, which, should he allow them one moment of license, would wreak upon him some terrible fatality. It was strangely frightful to the young man's imagination, to see this air of insecurity in a person cultivating a garden, that most simple and innocent of human toils, and which had been alike the joy and labor of the unfallen parents of the race. Was this garden, then, the Eden of the present world?—and this man, with such a perception of harm in what his own hands caused to grow, was he the Adam?

The distrustful gardener, while plucking away the dead leaves or pruning the too luxuriant growth of the shrubs, defended his hands with a pair of thick gloves. Nor were these his only armor. When, in his walk through the garden, he came to the magnificent plant that hung its purple gems beside the marble fountain, he placed a kind of mask over his mouth and nostrils, as if all this beauty did but conceal a deadlier malice. But finding his task still too dangerous, he drew back, removed the mask, and called loudly, but in the infirm voice of a person affected with inward disease:

"Beatrice!—Beatrice!"

"Here am I, my father! What would you?" cried a rich and youthful voice from the window of the opposite house; a voice as rich as a tropical sunset, and which made Giovanni, though he knew not why, think of deep hues of purple or crimson, and of perfumes heavily delectable.—"Are you in the garden?"

"Yes, Beatrice," answered the gardener, "and I need your help."

Soon there emerged from under a sculptured portal the figure of a young girl, arrayed with as much richness of taste as the most splendid of the flowers, beautiful as the day, and with a bloom so deep and vivid that one shade more would have been too much. She looked redundant with life, health, and energy. Yet Giovanni's fancy must have grown morbid, while he looked down into the garden; for the impression which the fair stranger made upon him was as if here were another flower, the human sister of those vegetable ones, as beautiful as they—more beautiful than the richest of them—but still to be touched only with a glove, nor to be approached without a mask. As Beatrice came down the garden-path, it was observable that she handled and inhaled the odor of several of the plants, which her father had most sedulously avoided.

"Here, Beatrice," said the latter,—"see how many needful offices require to be done to our chief treasure. Yet, shattered as I am, my life might pay the penalty of approaching it so closely as circumstances demand. Henceforth, I fear, this plant must be consigned to your sole charge."

"And gladly will I undertake it," cried again the rich tones of the young lady, as she bent towards the magnificent plant, and opened her arms as if to embrace it. "Yes, my sister, my splendor, it shall be Beatrice's task to nurse and serve thee; and thou shalt reward her with thy kisses and perfume breath, which to her is as the breath of life!"

Then, with all the tenderness in her manner that was so strikingly expressed in her words, she busied herself with such attentions as the plant seemed to require; and Giovanni, at his lofty window, rubbed his eyes, and almost doubted whether it were a girl tending her favorite flower, or one sister performing the duties of affection to another. The scene soon terminated. Whether Doctor Rappaccini had finished his labors in the garden, or that his watchful eye had caught the stranger's face, he now took his daughter's arm and retired. Night was already closing in; oppressive exhalations seemed to proceed from the plants, and steal upward past the open window; and Giovanni, closing the lattice, went to his couch, and dreamed of a rich flower and beautiful girl. Flower and maiden were different and yet the same, and fraught with some strange peril in either shape.

213. In paragraph 1, the narrator, Giovanni, is "impressed . . . disagreeably" by

   (A) the advanced age of the gardener.
   (B) the ugliness of the plants in the garden.
   (C) the gardener's fear of touching his own plants.
   (D) his own imagination.

214. In paragraph 1, the word *demeanor* most likely means

   (A) "visage."
   (B) "dexterity."
   (C) "cautiousness."
   (D) "disposition."

215. In lines 6–12 of paragraph 1, it can be inferred that

(A) the gardener does not know how to care for the flowers.

(B) this is not the real gardener, and he is trespassing.

(C) the gardener is careful because he knows the plants are dangerous.

(D) Giovanni knows the plants are poisonous.

216. All of the following quotes are supporting evidence for the previous answer *except*

(A) "the distrustful gardener."

(B) "defended his hands with thick gloves."

(C) "pruning the too luxuriant growth."

(D) "his task still too dangerous."

217. Giovanni's description of Beatrice's voice as "a voice as rich as a tropical sunset" is an example of

(A) personification.

(B) simile.

(C) analogy.

(D) metaphor.

218. Giovanni's first impression of Beatrice is that

(A) she is very young to be working in a garden.

(B) she is almost too beautiful to be real.

(C) she is rich and spoiled.

(D) she is dangerous.

219. In paragraph 6, the word *morbid* most nearly means

(A) "exaggerated."

(B) "obsessed."

(C) "expansive."

(D) "sinister."

220. What observation does Giovanni make in paragraph 6 that disturbs him?

(A) Beatrice looks like a flower.

(B) Beatrice touches the flowers and plants without gloves.

(C) The old gardener removes his mask.

(D) Beatrice tries to hide her beauty.

221. What might be inferred about Giovanni's personality from this passage?

(A) He believes in love at first sight.

(B) He does not like gardening.

(C) He has a vivid imagination.

(D) He is very observant.

222. The word *consigned* most likely means

(A) "disposed."
(B) "quarantined."
(C) "transferred."
(D) "mutated."

223. The word *fraught* most nearly means

(A) "burdened."
(B) "antagonized."
(C) "quarrelsome."
(D) "fatal."

224. The final sentence of the passage foreshadows

(A) Giovanni falling in love with Beatrice.
(B) that Beatrice will be a danger to Giovanni.
(C) that the flower is poisonous and kills Beatrice.
(D) that Giovanni kills the poisonous flower to save Beatrice.

Passage 20

President Barack Obama's Second Inaugural Speech, 2009

Forty-four Americans have now taken the presidential oath. The words have been spoken during rising tides of prosperity and the still waters of peace. Yet, every so often, the oath is taken amidst gathering clouds and raging storms. At these moments, America has carried on not simply because of the skill or vision of those in high office, but because we, the people, have remained faithful to the ideals of our forebears and true to our founding documents.

So it has been; so it must be with this generation of Americans.

That we are in the midst of crisis is now well understood. Our nation is at war against a far-reaching network of violence and hatred. Our economy is badly weakened, a consequence of greed and irresponsibility on the part of some, but also our collective failure to make hard choices and prepare the nation for a new age. Homes have been lost, jobs shed, businesses shuttered. Our health care is too costly, our schools fail too many—and each day brings further evidence that the ways we use energy strengthens our adversaries and threatens our planet. These are the indicators of crisis, subject to data and statistics. Less measurable, but no less profound, is a sapping of confidence across our land; a nagging fear that America's decline is inevitable, that the next generation must lower its sights.

Today I say to you that the challenges we face are real. They are serious and they are many. They will not be met easily or in a short span of time. But know this America: They will be met.

On this day, we gather because we have chosen hope over fear, unity of purpose over conflict and discord. On this day, we come to proclaim an end to the petty grievances and false promises, the recriminations and worn-out dogmas that for far too long have strangled our politics. We remain a young nation. But in the words of Scripture, the time has come to set aside childish things. The time has come to reaffirm our enduring spirit; to choose our better history; to carry forward that precious gift, that noble idea passed on from generation to generation: the God-given promise that all are equal, all are free, and all deserve a chance to pursue their full measure of happiness.

In reaffirming the greatness of our nation we understand that greatness is never a given. It must be earned. Our journey has never been one of shortcuts or settling for less. It has not been the path for the faint-hearted, for those that prefer leisure over work, or seek only the pleasures of riches and fame. Rather, it has been the risk-takers, the doers, the makers of things—some celebrated, but more often men and women obscure in their labor—who have carried us up the long rugged path towards prosperity and freedom.

For us, they packed up their few worldly possessions and traveled across oceans in search of a new life.

For us, they toiled in sweatshops and settled the West; endured the lash of the whip and plowed the hard earth.

For us, they fought and died, in places like Concord and Gettysburg; Normandy and Khe Sanh.

Time and again these men and women struggled and sacrificed and worked till their hands were raw so that we might live a better life. They saw America as bigger than the sum of our individual ambitions; greater than all the differences of birth or wealth or faction.

This is the journey we continue today. We remain the most prosperous, powerful nation on Earth. Our workers are no less productive than when this crisis began. Our minds are no less inventive, our goods and services no less needed than they were last week or last month or last year. Our capacity remains undiminished. But our time of standing pat, of protecting narrow interests and putting off unpleasant decisions—that time has surely passed. Starting today, we must pick ourselves up, dust ourselves off, and begin again the work of remaking America.

225. The phrase "gathering clouds and raging storms" most likely refers to

(A) the poetic nature of the speech.
(B) the war on terror.
(C) the weather.
(D) the difficult challenges America faces.

226. The word *prosperity* most likely means

(A) "calamity."
(B) "success."
(C) "poverty."
(D) "propensity."

227. "The time has come to reaffirm our enduring spirit; to choose our better history; to carry forward that precious gift, that noble idea passed on from generation to generation: the God-given promise that all are equal, all are free, and all deserve a chance to pursue their full measure of happiness" implies that

- (A) America is successful because its people still believe in the Declaration of Independence and the Constitution.
- (B) America has great presidents.
- (C) Americans are loyal.
- (D) the American dream is the greatest dream someone can have.

228. "So it has been; so it must be" is an example of

- (A) simile.
- (B) parallelism.
- (C) repetition.
- (D) paradox.

229. The main point of paragraph 3 is

- (A) to blame previous presidents for America's failures.
- (B) to present examples of the struggles America is facing.
- (C) to complain how expensive it will be to solve America's problems.
- (D) to comfort the American people that the nation is not failing.

230. The use of the word *inevitable* in paragraph 3 most likely means

- (A) "catastrophic."
- (B) "inexorable."
- (C) "fated."
- (D) "invincible."

231. The word *dogma* most nearly means

- (A) "doctrine."
- (B) "documents."
- (C) "religion."
- (D) "hypocrisy."

232. President Obama's purpose for speaking about the struggles and failures of America in paragraph 3 is most likely

- (A) to provide a contrast of what happened during the previous presidency to what he hopes to accomplish.
- (B) to prove he sympathizes with what the average American person is going through.
- (C) to show he is paying attention to the condition of life in the country and the people who are experiencing it.
- (D) to educate the public on what is really happening in the country.

233. The following quote, "The time has come to reaffirm our enduring spirit; to choose our better history; to carry forward that precious gift, that noble idea passed on from generation to generation: the God-given promise that all are equal, all are free, and all deserve a chance to pursue their full measure of happiness," implies that

(A) time is running out to make America great again.

(B) America's success or failure is the choice of the American people.

(C) it is time to stop pretending bad things have not happened in America's history.

(D) the American people must choose to work together to save the American dream and the ideas of freedom and happiness.

234. In paragraph 6, the word *reaffirming* most nearly means

(A) "kindling."

(B) "validating."

(C) "undermining."

(D) "proclaiming."

235. Paragraphs 7–9 serve to emphasize the idea that

(A) taking too many risks will cause a loss of wealth and fame.

(B) America can only be great if the workers push themselves harder.

(C) America's greatness was earned through hard work and sacrifice.

(D) too many people have died trying to make America successful.

236. The main purpose of President Obama's speech was most likely

(A) to remind the country about the failures of the previous administration.

(B) to express gratitude for the loyalty and sacrifice of previous generations.

(C) to promise his presidency will make positive change for the American people.

(D) to rally the American people.

Passage 21

A hoarder is someone who is unable or unwilling to throw items away, and the disposal of items causes them considerable anguish. When people hoard a massive number of objects, it takes over the livable spaces of their home. As the collection grows, they are unable to do simple, quotidian activities such as cooking a meal or watching TV. Sometimes the hoarding is so severe that portions of their homes become inaccessible.

But among the many problems that such behavior brings about, the most significant are the health risks. Once hallways and windows are blocked, hoarders are at risk of dying in a fire, as they no longer have a clear path of evacuation.

Piles that are stacked up high can fall on top of the homeowner, or a person trying to climb over a stack of objects can experience a fall. There is also the problem of poor sanitation. Areas where food cannot be properly cleaned begin to attract roaches and vermin, and bathrooms that are full of many possessions can no longer be washed and scoured. Pets living in the home of a hoarder can also suffer health problems and risk injury or neglect due to the conditions of the home. The animals may be exposed to dangerous objects or poisonous chemicals that are not properly stored.

Unfortunately, the severity of the problem can escalate for two reasons. One is that because the behavior progresses behind closed doors, people can amass collections of objects for years before friends or family members become aware of the problem. Technology enables hoarding by removing some of the challenges that a person would face having to shop in real life. The ability to make purchases and other transactions online allows items to be delivered right to customers without the potential obstacle of transportation.

Additionally, it becomes easier to spend more than you can afford when paying with a credit card. Hoarding can cause significant financial debt. The side effects of hoarding can cause irreparable damage to relationships, especially if the people involved cohabitate, because they may disagree that it is a problem, argue about paying bills and spending money, or disagree about the use of space in the home. Another challenge is that hoarders often do not recognize that they have a problem, and will continue to live in denial until they get professional help.

When attempting to make a diagnosis, psychologists do not categorize hoarding as a disorder in itself. Instead, it is often seen as a symptom of obsessive-compulsive disorder (OCD), depression, anxiety, or attention-deficit hyperactivity disorder (ADHD). Hoarding items may be one way for a person to feel more secure and prepared for an unexpected situation. The mental health community has only recently begun an intensive study of hoarding, and more research is needed in order to understand its causes and find effective treatment.

237. With which of the following statements would the author most likely agree?
    (A) The most significant problem caused by hoarding is the economic burden.
    (B) Luckily, hoarded items cannot be stacked higher than a person's head.
    (C) Hoarding is a debilitating behavioral condition.
    (D) Psychologists do not believe that hoarding is a real problem.

238. Which of the following statements most supports the author's conclusion?
    (A) Hoarding is more prevalent in older men.
    (B) People who hoard usually do not have other obsessive-compulsive symptoms.
    (C) Mental health professionals are not doing enough to make the public aware of hoarding.
    (D) Hoarding is a relatively new syndrome for the mental health community to address.

239. As used in paragraph 1, the word *quotidian* most nearly means

(A) "commonplace."

(B) "abnormal."

(C) "piquant."

(D) "unbroken."

240. The first paragraph mostly serves to

(A) warn the public about obsessive-compulsive disorder.

(B) illustrate how infrequent hoarding is.

(C) introduce the problem of hoarding.

(D) explain the connection between hoarding and depression.

241. As used in paragraph 3, the word *escalate* most nearly means

(A) "exploit."

(B) "delineate."

(C) "burnish."

(D) "intensify."

242. All of the following are health hazards that result from hoarding *except*

(A) physical injury.

(B) insect infestation.

(C) bacteria buildup.

(D) credit card debt.

243. The author would most likely disagree with which statement?

(A) Technology enables hoarding.

(B) Hoarding is a disability.

(C) To stop a hoarder, just throw away all the stuff.

(D) Relationships can be impacted by hoarding.

244. In paragraph 4, the word *irreparable* most nearly means

(A) "irreplaceable."

(B) "permanent."

(C) "egregious."

(D) "superficial."

245. According to paragraph 4, the following statements are all possible consequences of hoarding *except*

(A) as long as you can afford it, it's not hoarding.

(B) it can create large amounts of debt.

(C) it can lead to arguments about money.

(D) it can cause relationship problems.

246. The main purpose of paragraph 5 is

(A) to define hoarding as a disease.

(B) to explain potential reasons for hoarding behavior.

(C) to illustrate the need for new treatments.

(D) to promote awareness of the dangers of hoarding.

247. In paragraph 4, the word *denial* most nearly means

(A) "rejection."

(B) "confirmation."

(C) "disillusion."

(D) "attrition."

248. Which of the following statements would make the most sense to add to the final paragraph?

(A) Friends and families should report suspicions of hoarding to a person's doctor.

(B) The negative effects of hoarding can ruin lives.

(C) Openly discussing hoarding behaviors can provide insight for doctors and researchers.

(D) Psychologists should diagnose hoarders with a disorder so they can receive better treatment.

Passage 22A

One controversial interaction that the fashion industry has with the public is the issue of "plus-size " fashion—from models to specialty boutiques—which has both its champions and detractors.

Advocates for plus-size fashion marketing say that it is a positive step for an industry that has been corrupted by a preference for models who sometimes do not even weigh 100 pounds. So in a literal sense, fashion models have traditionally been nearly half the size of the average American woman. Supporters of plus-size fashion say that the fashion industry—and by extension, the media—bombards people with images of women that are unhealthy and not at all realistic. Therefore, plus-size clothes and models are a step in the right direction.

However, others say that the term *plus size* in the fashion industry is a misnomer. Many times, the plus-size model is only a size 6, and even the largest model in the industry is still only about a size 10. Yet the average American woman is a size 14. So although the efforts of a number of high-profile designers to include "larger" models and bigger sizes in their recent collections are commendable, they are still not representative of reality.

All these opponents, however, are still missing the most important point—plus-size fashion marketing should not exist at all. The proliferation of plus-size fashion clothing, as well as plus-size women being championed as role models, will only result in the acceptance of obesity in our society.

This is tremendously damaging, as obesity rates in the United States are on a continuous upswing. The industry is responsible for how it markets products and images to society, and therefore should only show images of people who are fit and trim.

Passage 22B

The specter of eating disorders in the fashion industry is an ever-present issue. Experts estimate that many models at top agencies are as much as 20 percent underweight. The World Health Organization considers a body mass index (BMI) value of 16 to be severe thinness, but many models are well below that figure. The pressure to remain this thin is why some models resort to anorexia and bulimia, and this pressure often trickles down to women in general because of images in the media.

It is not hard to see why these disorders are pernicious—and so often deadly. Model Ana Carolina Reston had a BMI of only 13 and weighed just 88 pounds at the time of her death at age 21 in 2006. That same year, model Isabelle Caro slipped into a coma after starving herself down to just 55 pounds.

In response to calls for more proactive measures, officials at some leading modeling events have implemented guidelines to encourage healthy body weights, such as not allowing models with a BMI lower than 18 to walk the runway.

Clearly, the question remains of whether modeling agencies and top design companies have the ethical responsibility to move away from the ultrathin appearance that characterizes the industry. However, it is not up to the industry to edit its message. It is up to the models' guardians to make sure they are eating properly, and up to parents of young women to help them have a healthy body image.

249. As used in Passage 22B, the word *specter* most nearly means

(A) "presence."
(B) "banshee."
(C) "opulence."
(D) "protrusion."

250. The author's primary purpose in writing Passage 22A is to

(A) discuss opinions about plus-size fashion.
(B) explain the history of fashion nomenclature.
(C) reveal the reasons behind US obesity rates.
(D) justify the existence of catwalk models.

251. The authors of the two passages would most likely disagree on

    (A) whether overweight people should be allowed to purchase designer clothes.

    (B) how common eating disorders are in the fashion industry.

    (C) whether the industry is responsible for how it markets products and images to society.

    (D) which designers should be allowed to place ads in magazines.

252. As used in paragraph 2 of Passage 22A, the word *bombards* most nearly means

    (A) "overwhelms."

    (B) "obfuscates."

    (C) "compromises."

    (D) "convulses."

253. The author's attitude toward plus-size marketing in Passage 22A can best be described as

    (A) "extravagant."

    (B) "conditional."

    (C) "subservient."

    (D) "antagonistic."

254. As used in paragraph 2 of Passage 22B, the word *pernicious* most nearly means

    (A) "bountiful."

    (B) "destructive."

    (C) "inexhaustible."

    (D) "antediluvian."

255. With which of the following statements would the author of Passage 22A most likely agree?

    (A) Today's most prolific designers are the best the industry has ever seen.

    (B) The fashion industry should emphasize a trim, athletic figure as the ideal body type.

    (C) Designers need to produce more products in American factories.

    (D) Designer knockoffs are a serious problem for the fashion industry.

256. As used in paragraph 3 of Passage 22B, the word *proactive* most nearly means

    (A) "inconceivable."

    (B) "energetic."

    (C) "capricious."

    (D) "neglectful."

257. Both passages mention the fact that the fashion industry

(A) has been avoiding the topic of eating disorders among runway models since the mid-1970s.

(B) in the United States is responsible for the abundance of plus-size models in Europe.

(C) has taken a number of steps to address inconsistencies in sizing for women, including changing to a measurement system, like men's clothing has.

(D) has been accused of portraying women's bodies through the media in ways that are harmful and unreasonable.

258. As used in paragraph 3 of Passage 22A, the word *misnomer* most nearly means

(A) "an unsuitable term."

(B) "a terrible insult."

(C) "an obvious lie."

(D) "a term of endearment."

259. In paragraph 3 of Passage 22B, the author suggests that

(A) agencies and designers should not be blamed for the eating behaviors of their models or of adolescents in society.

(B) models with a BMI lower than 18 should no longer be allowed to walk any runways in European and Asian shows.

(C) the BMI of many models in the fashion industry is well below the figure that the World Health Organization considers to be severe thinness.

(D) eating disorders are not an issue that agencies and designers need to take seriously at the moment.

260. What evidence would make the conclusion of Passage 22B stronger?

(A) Current statistics of the obesity rates in the United States and the increase of plus-sized advertising

(B) Quotes from models with eating disorders

(C) Surveys asking people how they feel about plus-size models and advertising

(D) Results from studies on the causes of obesity in the United States

Passage 23

Adapted from Saki's "The Interlopers"

The two enemies stood glaring at one another for a long, silent moment. Each had a rifle in his hand, each had hate in his heart and murder uppermost in his mind.

The chance had come to give full play to the passions of a lifetime. But a man who has been brought up under the code of a restraining civilization cannot easily nerve himself to shoot down his neighbor in cold blood and without a word spoken, except for an offence against his hearth and honor. And before the moment of hesitation had given way to action a deed of Nature's own violence overwhelmed them both. A fierce shriek of the storm had been answered by a splitting crash over their heads, and ere they could leap aside a mass of falling beech tree had thundered down on them. Ulrich von Gradwitz found himself stretched on the ground, one arm numb beneath him and the other held almost as helplessly in a tight tangle of forked branches, while both legs were pinned beneath the fallen mass. His heavy shooting-boots had saved his feet from being crushed to pieces, but if his fractures were not as serious as they might have been, at least it was evident that he could not move from his present position till someone came to release him. The descending twig had slashed the skin of his face, and he had to wink away some drops of blood from his eyelashes before he could take in a general view of the disaster. At his side, so near that under ordinary circumstances he could almost have touched him, lay Georg Znaeym, alive and struggling, but obviously as helplessly pinioned down as himself. All round them lay a thick-strewn wreckage of splintered branches and broken twigs.

Relief at being alive and exasperation at his captive plight brought a strange medley of pious thank-offerings and sharp curses to Ulrich's lips. Georg, who was nearly blinded with the blood that trickled across his eyes, stopped his struggling for a moment to listen and then gave a short, snarling laugh.

"So you're not killed, as you ought to be, but you're caught, anyway," he cried; "caught fast. Ho, what a jest, Ulrich von Gradwitz snared in his stolen forest. There's real justice for you!"

And he laughed again, mockingly and savagely.

"I'm caught in my own forest land," retorted Ulrich. "When my men come to release us, you will wish, perhaps, that you were in a better plight than caught poaching on a neighbor's land, shame on you."

Georg was silent for a moment; then he answered quietly:

"Are you sure that your men will find much to release? I have men, too, in the forest tonight, close behind me, and *they* will be here first and do the releasing. When they drag me out from under these cursed branches it won't need much clumsiness on their part to roll this mass of trunk right over on the top of you. Your men will find you dead under a fallen beech tree. For form's sake I shall send my condolences to your family."

"It is a useful hint," said Ulrich fiercely. "My men had orders to follow in ten minutes time, seven of which must have gone by already, and when they get me out—I will remember the hint. Only as you will have met your death poaching on my lands, I don't think I can decently send any message of condolence to your family."

"Good," snarled Georg, "good. We fight this quarrel out to the death, you and I and our foresters, with no cursed interlopers to come between us. Death and damnation to you, Ulrich von Gradwitz."

"The same to you, Georg Znaeym, forest thief, game snatcher."

Both men spoke with the bitterness of possible defeat before them, for each knew that it might be long before his men would seek him out or find him; it was a bare matter of chance which party would arrive first on the scene.

Both had now given up the useless struggle to free themselves from the mass of wood that held them down; Ulrich limited his endeavors to an effort to bring his one partially free arm near enough to his outer coat-pocket to draw out his wine-flask. Even when he had accomplished that operation, it was long before he could manage the unscrewing of the stopper or get any of the liquid down his throat. But what a Heaven-sent draught it seemed! It was an open winter, and little snow had fallen as yet; hence the captives suffered less from the cold than might have been the case at that season of the year. Nevertheless, the wine was warming and reviving to the wounded man, and he looked across with something like a throb of pity to where his enemy lay, just keeping the groans of pain and weariness from crossing his lips.

"Could you reach this flask if I threw it over to you?" asked Ulrich suddenly; "there is good wine in it, and one may as well be as comfortable as one can. Let us drink, even if tonight one of us dies."

"No, I can scarcely see anything; there is so much blood caked round my eyes," said Georg, "and in any case I don't drink wine with an enemy."

Ulrich was silent for a few minutes, and lay listening to the weary screeching of the wind. An idea was slowly forming and growing in his brain, an idea that gained strength every time that he looked across at the man who was fighting so grimly against pain and exhaustion. In the pain and languor that Ulrich himself was feeling the old fierce hatred seemed to be dying down.

"Neighbor," he said presently, "do as you please if your men come first. It was a fair compact. But as for me, I've changed my mind. If my men are the first to come you shall be the first to be helped, as though you were my guest. We have quarreled like devils all our lives over this stupid strip of forest, where the trees can't even stand upright in a breath of wind. Lying here tonight, thinking, I've come to think we've been rather fools. There are better things in life than getting the better of a boundary dispute. Neighbor, if you will help me to bury the old quarrel, I—I will ask you to be my friend."

261. Which of the following best summarizes a major theme of the selection?

(A) Good fences make good neighbors.

(B) Some feuds just cannot be resolved and it is better to leave them be.

(C) No one "owns" land because nature is indifferent to human ownership.

(D) There is no purpose in holding on to petty grudges.

262. Which of the following quotes best supports the answer to the previous question?

(A) "But a man who has been brought up under the code of a restraining civilization cannot easily nerve himself to shoot down his neighbor in cold blood and without word spoken, except for an offence against his hearth and honor."

(B) "And before the moment of hesitation had given way to action a deed of Nature's own violence overwhelmed them both."

(C) "When my men come to release us you will wish, perhaps, that you were in a better plight than caught poaching on a neighbor's land, shame on you."

(D) "Lying here tonight, thinking, I've come to think we've been rather fools. There are better things in life than getting the better of a boundary dispute."

263. Which of the following statements best describes the relationship between Ulrich and Georg?

(A) Because of their families' feud, they both consider each other enemies and trespassers.

(B) They were once friends, but after the court's decision, they turned against one another.

(C) They wanted to end their feud but couldn't because of their families.

(D) Though Georg knows Ulrich is the forest's legal property owner, he continues to trespass and hunt illegally.

264. The phrase "the code of a restraining civilization" most likely refers to

(A) the rules of war.
(B) laws and regulations.
(C) a code for a secret society.
(D) the rituals of an ancient civilization.

265. In paragraph 1, the word *pinioned* most likely means

(A) "lacerated."
(B) "betrayed."
(C) "immobilized."
(D) "crushed."

266. Which of the following statement best describes irony of Georg and Ulrich's predicament?

(A) Ulrich is not hurt as badly as Georg.
(B) Both men say they are not alone in the woods.
(C) Each man thinks he will be rescued first and leave the other man dead.
(D) They wanted to kill each other and now they are trapped and seriously injured together.

267. In paragraph 10, the word *interlopers* most likely means

(A) "forest animals."
(B) "family members."
(C) "intruders."
(D) "apparitions."

268. The main conflict in the passage is

(A) man versus nature.
(B) man versus self.
(C) man versus man.
(D) man versus God.

269. Based on the previous answer, which of the following choices is an example of the conflict?

(A) Ulrich prays for rescue, but no one arrives.
(B) Georg and Ulrich have a long-standing feud and hate each other.
(C) The men are in danger of freezing to death in the woods.
(D) Georg is conflicted about forgiving Ulrich for getting him into this situation.

270. In the final paragraph, the word *compact* most likely means

(A) "compressed."
(B) "agreement."
(C) "trade."
(D) "bounty."

PART 2

Writing and Language

CHAPTER 4

Set 1 Writing and Language Questions

Passage 1

The sign on the door says "No Pets Allowed" and in smaller letters, toward the bottom, "Service Animals Welcome." But a dog is a dog, isn't it? Not for someone with a disability. A service dog is not a pet. Long before the term *service dog* was coined, dogs have been pets, hunters, protectors, and guides. [271] Today, dogs have roles in the police force, the military, hospitals and nursing homes, and other public service fields, including serving individuals with a variety of disabilities.

According to the Americans with Disabilities Act of 1990, a service dog is defined as "any guide dog, signal dog, or other animal individually trained to provide assistance to an individual with a disability." Prior to the 1960s, most service dogs were guide ("seeing-eye") dogs for blind people. In 1976, the National Education for Assistance Dogs Services began training and using dogs as hearing assistants for the deaf. In 1996, they began pairing service dogs with children diagnosed with autism, and in 2012, with people suffering from post-traumatic stress disorder. In fact, psychiatric disabilities are fourth, behind blindness, mobility impaired, and deafness, with the highest demands for service dogs.
272
273

Everyone knows dogs are very smart. <u>They can be trained to sniff for guns, explosives, and drugs. They can be trained to find survivors of natural disasters</u>
₂₇₄
<u>or dead bodies covered in rubble and wreckage.</u> The training required for service dogs is very hard work for both the dog and the trainer. It can take 18 to 24 months to train a service dog, and over the lifetime, training and care can cost up to $24,000. These are some of the basic tasks a service dog might have to <u>perform: open doors</u>, retrieve objects, alert or <u>summon</u> a person from another
₂₇₅ ₂₇₆
room, learn a special bark to use with a speaker phone in case of an emergency, signal owner for fire or burglar alarms, offer mobility assistance, and lead emergency help to an owner's location. Service dogs for psychiatric disabilities have more specialized training to guide a disoriented handler, <u>providing</u> tactile
₂₇₇
support during an anxiety attack, identify and alert handler to hallucinations, search a room, and interrupt or redirect a person engaged in trigger behaviors. Dogs can even be trained to signal <u>they're</u> owner about an oncoming seizure in
₂₇₈
an epileptic or when a diabetic person needs to take insulin.

[1] Due to the intense training needed <u>in</u> a successful service dog, it is
₂₇₉
important to pick the right dog for the job. [2] <u>Most training begins within</u>
₂₈₀
<u>the first week a puppy is born.</u> [3] When picking the breed, a person should consider their lifestyle to determine what size, energy level, and maintenance level is appropriate for them. [4] The temperament of the puppy is also very important because it will not grow out of those qualities. [5] A service dog needs to be calm, focused, and confident. [6] It would not be good if the dog was easily scared or distracted. [7] A service dog should also be trainable and intelligent, but not a breed that gets bored easily because it will be doing the same activities every day.

Approximately 500,000 service, therapy, and support dogs were reported working in the United States in 2016. There will always be a demand for high

quality dogs and the dedicated, caring people who <u>train them. But they</u> enable
281
people with a variety of disabilities to lead safe, healthy, and productive lives that
might otherwise be inaccessible.

271. Should the writer change sentence 1 to improve clarity?

(A) No change
(B) Today, dogs work with the police, military, in hospitals and nursing homes, and as service dogs to people with a variety of disabilities.
(C) Today, dogs have roles in the police force, the military, hospitals and nursing homes, and they also work in public service fields, including serving individuals with a variety of disabilities.
(D) Police, military, hospitals and nursing homes all use dogs in their work, and people with disabilities also use dogs for assistance.

272. Should the writer make any changes to sentence 2?

(A) No change
(B) Prior to the 1960s; most service dogs
(C) Prior to the 1960s most service dogs,
(D) Most service dogs before the 1960s,

273. Choose the best option.

(A) No change
(B) mobility impairments
(C) physically impaired
(D) handicapped

274. Should the writer make changes to improve conciseness and clarity?

(A) No change
(B) They can be trained to sniff for guns, explosives, and drugs, and they can be trained to find survivors of natural disasters or dead bodies covered in rubble and wreckage.
(C) They can be trained to sniff for guns, explosives, drugs, and to find survivors of natural disasters or dead bodies covered in rubble and wreckage.
(D) They can be training for many tasks: sniffing for guns, explosives, and drugs, or finding survivors or dead bodies.

275.

(A) No change
(B) perform open doors
(C) perform; open door's
(D) perform to open doors

276.

    (A) No change
    (B) retrieve
    (C) accompany
    (D) recover

277.

    (A) No change
    (B) provides
    (C) provided
    (D) provide

278.

    (A) No change
    (B) their
    (C) its
    (D) there

279.

    (A) No change
    (B) with
    (C) for
    (D) by

280. To make this paragraph the most logical, sentence 2 should be placed

    (A) where it is.
    (B) before sentence 1.
    (C) deleted from the paragraph.
    (D) after sentence 3.

281. Which choice most effectively combines the two sentences at the underlined portion?

    (A) train them but they
    (B) train them, and they
    (C) train them, and these dogs
    (D) train them, but those dogs

282. Which sentence would provide more supporting evidence for the final paragraph?

  (A) The average salary of a service dog trainer is from $26,000 per year up to $48,000 per year, making it a good career option.

  (B) The number of adults in the United States reporting disabilities increased by 3.4 million between 1999 and 2005 and continues to rise.

  (C) Ninety-two percent of blind people report being more active after they received a guide dog.

  (D) An increase in service dog fraud hurts people with real disabilities.

Passage 2

The world is becoming a smaller and smaller place. Not physically, but the global community is more interconnected than ever thanks to technology and a myriad
283
of transportation options. People are moving, and they are doing so on an international scale. Immigration and emigration, job opportunities, educational experiences, and mixed culture families are creating more diversity than ever, and sometimes it becomes difficult to trace the heritage that makes you, well,
284
you. The new trend of at home DNA tests is capitalizing on people's intrinsic
285
desires to know more about who they are and where they come from, and it is a booming business.

AncestryDNA is one of the largest commercial DNA test companies, with a database of over 2.5 million registered users and growing faster than any other company. They sold 1.5 million kits in 2017 on Black Friday. AncestryDNA is one of the most popular testing companies because of its elaborate marketing strategies and additional services offered, like family tree integration and shared DNA matches within the database. [286] If a person is looking for something more reliable, 23andMe is the way to go. With the most reliable ethnicity estimates, medical traits reports, and a chromosome browser. 23andMe offers
287
more in-depth knowledge about an individual person's DNA, not just general genealogy. Technology is making DNA more comprehensible and accessible

to <u>the average person and discovery</u> of DNA and its connections to hereditary
₂₈₈
genetics began about 150 years ago.

Deoxyribonucleic acid, DNA, research dates back to <u>the 1860s, but studies</u>
₂₈₉
linking DNA to society's current concepts of it really began in 1950 when Erwin

Chargaff proved DNA was species specific. Incredibly, human beings worldwide

share 99 percent of the same DNA! In 1953, the double helix structure

<u>was discovered, enabling</u> researchers to see the DNA strands mapping out
₂₉₀
chromosomal pairs. These chromosomes contain the genes that determine the

biological heritage of an individual that can reveal ethnic heritage and discover

familial relationships, predispositions for genetic disorders, risk factors for

health, and other productive applications, including solving crimes. But all this

knowledge may not lead to the same excited consumers seen in the commercial.

There are a number of possible consequences to DNA discoveries that are not so

happy.

[1] First, identified ethnic origins can be misleading, as regions and countries

have changed names and boundaries over the centuries. [2] <u>What a country</u>

<u>is today might not be where a person's ancestors trace back to hundreds of</u>
₂₉₁
<u>years ago</u>. [3] Second, although these tests can reveal genetic health risks for

Parkinson's disease or Alzheimer's, there is no guarantee a person will develop it,

and the emotional strain of thinking about it could have a serious impact on a

person's life. [4] Genetic testing for the BRCA gene can tell a woman if she is at

risk for breast cancer, but many women who are diagnosed test negative for the

gene. [5] <u>Additionally</u>, though not often, some people discover things they wish
₂₉₂
they hadn't, like mistaken paternity or evidence of unexpected relatives.

[6] The creation of centralized DNA databases also carries the danger that private

information might leak out and be used for genetic and ethnic identification and

potential discrimination.

The ability to test our DNA at home and discover more information about who we are and where we come from is an exciting opportunity. The information learned has the potential to improve the quality of lives, identify and cure diseases, reconnect long-lost relatives, and give identities to people who may have no idea about their family's heritage. But consumers should also be aware of the possible risks involved, and carefully research the privacy policies of these at-home tests to protect themselves and their personal information. 293

283. The following revision would make the introductory sentences more concise.
- (A) No change
- (B) The global community is smaller than ever thanks to technology and transportation.
- (C) The global community is more interconnected than ever because of advances in technology.
- (D) Transportation and communication have made the global community smaller than ever.

284.
- (A) No change
- (B) sometimes it is difficult to trace your heritage
- (C) it can be difficult to trace
- (D) tracing that heritage can be difficult.

285.
- (A) No change
- (B) are
- (C) was
- (D) were

286. Which option best maintains the flow of the paragraph?
- (A) No change
- (B) 23andMe offers more in-depth knowledge about an individual's DNA. They have the most reliable ethnicity estimates, medical traits reports, and a chromosome browser.
- (C) For the most reliable ethnicity estimates, medical traits reports, and a chromosome browser, 23andMe offers more in-depth knowledge about an individual's DNA.
- (D) For more in-depth knowledge, 23andMe offers the most reliable ethnicity estimates, medical traits reports, and a chromosome browser.

287. Based on the previous answer, should the author delete the following sentence from the paragraph? "If a person is looking for something more reliable, 23andMe is the way to go."

    (A) No, because it is a good transition to discussing a new company

    (B) No, because it emphasizes 23andMe is better than AncestryDNA

    (C) Yes, because it is an opinion, not a fact

    (D) Yes, because all of the information is stated in another sentence

288.

    (A) No change

    (B) the average person, and the discovery of DNA

    (C) average people, but the discovery of DNA

    (D) average people, and the discovery of DNA

289.

    (A) No change

    (B) the 1860s, but studies

    (C) the 1860's but studies,

    (D) the 1860s' but, studies

290.

    (A) No change

    (B) were discovered enabling

    (C) did discover, enabling

    (D) has discovered enabling

291. Which option for sentence 2 best clarifies the first sentence in paragraph 3?

    (A) No change

    (B) Many ethnicities no longer exist in today's world so they could not be located by modern geography.

    (C) A person's ethnicity might trace back to a country or region that no longer exists on a modern map, or their ethnicity might be connected to a modern country that has been recently formed or renamed.

    (D) A person's ancestors might trace back to a country that existed hundreds of years ago.

292.

    (A) No change

    (B) Finally

    (C) Furthermore

    (D) Occasionally

293. Which sentence would strengthen the conclusion?

(A) DNA testing should be conducted by medical professionals only until appropriate security measures are in place to protect people.

(B) People need to realize DNA testing companies are more interested in making money than in the privacy of their customers.

(C) The emotional risks of taking a DNA test should be understood, and companies should provide support to the customers after the test results are distributed.

(D) In order for DNA testing companies, like AncestryDNA and 23andMe, to maintain their current success, they need to provide clear, detailed information about how they protect their customers' results, secure their databases against hackers, and offer follow-up services for the emotional component of the process.

Number of People Tested by Company

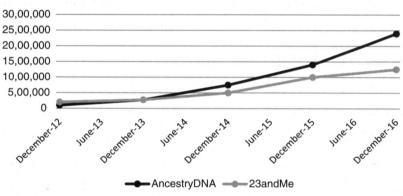

294. Which choice does not reflect information shown on the graph?

(A) Both companies started testing at the same time.

(B) AncestryDNA more than doubled the size of its database from 2015 to 2016.

(C) AncestryDNA tested almost twice the amount of people that 23andMe tested in 2016.

(D) Both companies tested the same amount of people in 2013.

295. Which paragraph would be strengthened using supporting evidence from this graph?

(A) Paragraph 1
(B) Paragraph 2
(C) Paragraph 4
(D) Paragraph 5

Passage 3

Central Park, in New York City, <u>is referred</u> to as "The Jewel of Manhattan" and
296
occupies a coveted 843 acres in the middle of one of the busiest cities in the
United States. <u>Its story began over 150 years ago. The New York State Legislature</u>
<u>enacted a law appropriating 700 acres of space in the middle of the island of</u>
297
<u>Manhattan to create America's first landscaped public park.</u> The legislature's
decision was based on the realization that a park would improve public health
and bring the people of New York together as a community. Citizens would be
more active and more social. 298

In 1858, a contest was held to determine the design of the park. Architects
Frederick Law Olmstead and Calvert Vaux, who later designed many other
famous New York public <u>Parks, were</u> the winners. Their design encompassed
299
a variety of landscapes including waterways and a pond, strategically placed
woodland areas, gently rolling paths, and even a sheep field where actual sheep
grazed! <u>Today these features contribute to the enjoyment of many Central Park</u>
300
<u>activities that residents and tourists enjoy.</u> In addition to paths for walking,
jogging, and bicycling, there are programs like Discovery Kits to explore the park,
a place to play board games, Keeping It Green programs for maintaining and
preserving the park, holiday events, concerts, and dog-friendly areas. <u>But</u> there are
301
shadows on Central Park's past; histories that most park goers are not aware of.

[1] When legislators decided to create Central Park, there was one thing in
<u>its</u> way; a whole village of people. [2] This area was known as Seneca Village,
302
a principal black settlement in New York City. [3] Very little is known about
the people who lived there, but when the area was cleared for the park, it was
home to an estimated 264 residents, black and Irish. [4] There were three known
churches, two schools, and three cemeteries. [5] <u>Even though residents were</u>

relocated, the cemeteries were never moved, and later excavations discovered
303
what might have been a former slave burial ground. [6] But these villagers were

not the only residents displaced. [7] A total of 1,600 people in the area were

relocated in order for the park to be constructed.

Another dark time for Central Park came after the Great Depression. With

no funds to maintain the park, landscaping began to decay, and structures fell
304
into disrepair. Citizens stopped using the park for socialization and exercise, and

incrementally, illegal activities and violence flooded into the park space, giving
305
it a negative reputation. The condition of the park deteriorated to the point

where the City of New York abdicated responsibility for the park and stopped

their efforts to clean it up. Finally, in 1974, a management study was conducted,
306
and action was taken to take back the park.

First, a CEO of Park Operations was selected. This person would have

complete control over decisions made to improve and maintain the park.

Second, a Central Park Board of Guardians was created to involve private citizens

in the use and development of the park. Campaigns took place in 1987, 1993,

and 2008 to raise money and restore the park to its former glory. Thanks to these

efforts, Central Park is once again the crown jewel it was meant to be; however,
307
people should not forget the sacrifices and struggles that went into making the

park what it is today.

296.

   (A) No change
   (B) was referred
   (C) refers
   (D) is referring

297. Which is the most effective and concise option for conveying the information?

(A) No change

(B) Over 150 years ago, The New York State Legislature enacted a law appropriating 700 acres of space in the middle of the island of Manhattan to create America's first landscaped public park.

(C) The New York Legislature enacted a law 150 years ago to create America's first landscaped public park, by appropriating 700 acres of space in the middle of Manhattan.

(D) Over 150 years ago, 700 acres of space was appropriated by the New York Legislature in the middle of Manhattan to create America's first landscaped public park.

298. The author is considering replacing the final sentence of the first paragraph. Should it be replaced?

(A) No, because it connects to the previous sentence

(B) No, but more information should be added about why citizens should be more active and more social

(C) Yes, because it does not enhance any information presented later in the essay

(D) Yes, because the final sentence of the first paragraph should relate to the final sentence in the last paragraph

299.

(A) No change

(B) parks were

(C) park's were,

(D) parks, were

300. The author is considering revising this sentence. Which of the following options should the write select?

(A) No change

(B) These features contribute to the enjoyment of many Central Park activities of residents and tourists.

(C) These features contribute to the enjoyment of many Central Park activities by residents and tourists.

(D) The enjoyment of many Central Park activities by residents and tourists is because of these features.

301.

(A) No change

(B) Although

(C) And

(D) Delete

302.

    (A) No change
    (B) their
    (C) it's
    (D) the

303. Which order would be the most effective for sentences [5], [6], and [7] to conclude the paragraph?

    (A) No change
    (B) [6], [7], then [5]
    (C) [6], [5], then [7]
    (D) [7], [6], then [5]

304.

    (A) No change
    (B) was decaying
    (C) decayed
    (D) decays

305.

    (A) No change
    (B) seeped
    (C) assimilated
    (D) interfered

306.

    (A) No change
    (B) their effort
    (C) its efforts
    (D) the efforts

307.

    (A) No change
    (B) to be; however, people
    (C) to be, however people
    (D) to be however people,

Passage 4

In the last decade, the United States has seen some of <u>its largest and most</u>
                                                  308
<u>costliest storms</u> in the last 100 years. With advanced technology enabling

meteorologists to predict storms days and even weeks in advance, terms like "superstorm" and "bombogenesis" are on the tips of everyone's tongues and sending communities into a frenzy of preparations. Superstorm Sandy in 2012 and Hurricane Harvey in 2011 are just two examples of large superstorms that ravaged areas of the United States. <u>Many factors influence the determination of a</u>

                                                                309

<u>superstorm.</u>

The difference between a hurricane (a tropical cyclone) and a winter cyclone is the energy source. Hurricanes draw their energy from warm water. <u>Winter cyclones that are not</u> the same as blizzards, draw their power from temperature

          310

contrasts in the atmosphere. This allows the storms to grow dramatically. Superstorm Sandy started as a hurricane that turned north and collided with a winter cyclone. The contrasting temperatures drew the storm inland and stretched it out. It was almost 1,000 miles across! <u>It also had the lowest recorded barometric pressure of any Atlantic storm in record history.</u> <u>A full moon during</u>

                                          311

<u>the storm resulted in record storm surges during high tide of 13.88 feet in</u>

                                            312

<u>New York.</u>

Although Sandy's size and impact <u>was devastating</u>, it was only the second

                                    313

most expensive and deadly storm to hit the United States in the last decade. Hurricane Harvey had over $100 billion in damages due to 51 inches of rain and devastating flooding, but the second fewest deaths of the five major hurricanes since 2010. Hurricane Matthew had the highest death toll due to its track across the small islands of the Caribbean that had little protection. It wasn't the storm surge or the rainfall alone that made it so devastating. Hovering over warm ocean waters, Hurricane Matthew sustained a category 5 rating. Flash floods and mudslides came down the mountains toward many small villages that lacked solid construction, and demolished them. Isolated locations meant a lack of clean water, food, medical support, and shelter for victims.

<u>As dangerous as superstorms are, the aftermath can be just as devastating.</u>
314
Flooding leads to water contamination as drainage and sewers run into lakes,

streams, and reservoirs. Harmful bacteria thrive in damp conditions and cause

mold growth in homes and buildings, which leads to respiratory problems.

After Hurricane Katrina, 105,000 condemned homes, built in the 1950s,

were <u>demolished, lead paint</u> leaching into the air, ground, and water of the
315
surrounding areas. The long-range consequences of this are still not known.

Delayed medical care in New York after Sandy led to 125 heart attacks, 35

strokes, and 70 deaths that might have been prevented.

This increase in severe large-scale storms raises a lot of questions about what

causes them and why they are increasing in frequency. Global warming is a

significant contributor according to climate scientists from Texas Tech who

were interviewed in 2012 by National Public Radio (NPR). Climate change is

contributing to the exacerbation of catastrophic weather events. Warmer ocean

temperatures lead to more evaporation and a 5 to 10 percent increase in rainfall

during precipitation events. <u>However these events become less regular leading</u>
316
to droughts and extended heat waves. Glaciers are melting, and rising sea levels

mean more damaging storm surges and more flooding. The United States has

4,514 miles of coastline with 20 percent at or below sea level making it very

vulnerable.

Superstorms are not going away, so it is more important than ever that

information about climate change and <u>its</u> impact on weather is understood at
317
a global level. Areas that have previously suffered significant losses need better

protection and better preparations for future storms. Scientists, urban planners,

and infrastructure specialists need to work together to ensure that people, homes,

and businesses can survive the wrath of future storms and continue to thrive in

their communities.

308.

    (A) No change
    (B) its largest and most costly storms
    (C) it's largest and costliest storms
    (D) its largest, costly storms

309. To improve the flow and organization of the passage, this sentence should be placed

    (A) where it is now.
    (B) as the first sentence of paragraph 2.
    (C) as the last sentence of paragraph 2.
    (D) deleted completely.

310.

    (A) No change
    (B) Winter cyclones, that are not
    (C) Winter cyclones, which are not
    (D) Winter cyclones are not

311. The author is considering deleting the underlined sentence. Should it be deleted?

    (A) No, because it states an important fact about the storm
    (B) Yes, because it does not state which storm the fact refers to
    (C) Yes, because it does not clearly relate to any other information given in the paragraph
    (D) No, because the information might be useful later on in the passage

312. Which choice provides the most concise version of sentence 9?

    (A) No change
    (B) A full moon, during the storm, resulted in record storm surges of 13.88 feet during high tide in New York.
    (C) In New York, a full moon resulted in record storm surges of 13.88 feet during high tide.
    (D) During the storm, a full moon resulted in record storm surges, in New York, of 13.88 feet.

313.

    (A) No change
    (B) has been devastating
    (C) were devastating
    (D) is devastating

314. Which option offers the most clear and concise introduction to paragraph 4?

   (A) No change

   (B) The aftermath can be as devastating as during the storm.

   (C) During the superstorm is not always as devastating as the aftermath.

   (D) The aftermath of a superstorm can be just as devastating as the storm itself.

315.

   (A) No change

   (B) demolished and lead paint

   (C) demolished, and lead paint

   (D) demolished: lead paint

316.

   (A) No change

   (B) However, these events become less regular leading

   (C) These events become less regular and lead

   (D) Drought and heat waves are caused by these events becoming less regular.

317.

   (A) No change

   (B) it's

   (C) their

   (D) our

	Hurricane Irma 2011	Hurricane Harvey 2011	Superstorm Sandy 2012	Hurricane Matthew 2016	Hurricane Maria 2017
Wind Gusts	185 mph	150 mph	95 mph	126 mph	155 mph
Rainfall	15 inches	51+ inches	12 inches	18 inches	20 inches
Storm Surge	15 feet	12.5 feet	8.9 feet	7.7 feet	9 feet
Death Toll	112	82	145	585	51
Cost to United States	$64 billion	$108 billion	$70.2 billion	$10 billion	$45 billion

Adapted from information provided by National Weather Service and Weather Prediction Center.

318. Based on the graph, which statement is the most accurate?

(A) The most dangerous storm surges occur with the highest wind gusts.

(B) There is no pattern to the characteristics of superstorms.

(C) Rainfall is the costliest factor of a superstorm.

(D) The severity of a superstorm is comprised of many factors that occur during and after the storm.

319. Which of the following statements from paragraph 2 is *not* supported by data from the graph?

(A) Hurricane Harvey had over $100 billion in damages due to 51 inches of rain

(B) Hurricane Matthew had the highest death toll due to its track across the small islands of the Caribbean that had little protection.

(C) [Sandy] . . . was only the second most expensive and deadly storm to hit the United States in the last decade.

(D) Flash floods and mudslides came down the mountains toward many small villages that lacked solid construction, and demolished them.

Passage 5

It seems like every big movie heist is accompanied by exciting technology and brilliantly savvy characters who use night vision and lasers, rappelling ropes, tiny drills, wireless headsets, computer hacking, and explosives to liberate priceless artifacts from well-guarded displays. And in the end, they always get caught. In real life, the biggest art heist in United States history is still unsolved, and the criminals had none of those high-tech gadgets. 320 On the night of March 18, 1990, two men dressed as police officers demanded entry into the Isabella Stewart Gardner Museum in Boston, Massachusetts, <u>threatening</u> the security
                                                                                                                321
guards with arrest, they handcuffed him, and made off with 13 works of art valued at over $600 million. 322

Isabella Stewart was born in New York in 1840, and she married Jack Gardner, a member of an upper-class New England family, and moved to Boston, Massachusetts. After the death of their son, at the advice of her physician, the Gardners traveled around the world to ease her depression.

During these travels, Isabella <u>begun</u> to seriously purchase art, and her collection

323

included paintings, drawings, tapestries, rare books, sculptures, and jewelry.

She befriended artists, authors, poets, and other creative thinkers. When they

returned home from their travels, she would host dinner parties, academic talks,

and other events to share her interests and art. Eventually, it became obvious that

their home was overflowing with their <u>treasures and</u> they dreamed of creating a

324

museum to share it with the public.

The death of her husband in 1898 <u>pushed</u> Isabella to make their dream of a

325

museum a reality. She chose an area of Boston known as the Fenway, famous for

its natural light and a nearby park system, and designed the building to reflect

a fifteenth-century Italian villa from one of her trips to Venice, Italy. Isabella

carefully planned each room—every detail, from the carpets to the wallpaper—

and a location for each of her treasures. Upon her death in 1924, Isabella's will

bequeathed $1 million for the continuation of her museum, with the condition

that nothing would be moved and no new work added, <u>not even to replace the</u>

326

<u>famous stolen artwork.</u>

It might not seem like 13 pieces out of a collection of 2,500 should be so

noteworthy, but they are historically significant and irreplaceable in the art

world. Rembrandt's painting *Christ in the Storm on the Sea of Galilee* and Manet's

Chez Tortoni were cut right out of <u>its</u> frames as they hung on the walls. The loss

327

of Vermeer's *The Concert* was extremely devastating to the museum because only

34 paintings by the artist are known to exist worldwide. Yet the thieves also took

artifacts that were lesser known, like a bronze-plated eagle and a Shang dynasty

vase. Over a span of 81 minutes, the thieves appropriated this odd assortment

of items and passed by numerous others that were more valuable, with no

discernible reason.

[1] Current museum security director, Anthony Amore, can now watch the original rooms and the 65,000 square feet of the museum's recent addition on banks of security monitors, ensuring there will be no repeat of the previous theft. [2] A $5 million reward is still being offered for the safe recovery of the stolen works, but in spite of hundreds of tips from the public and several theories by the FBI, no trace has ever appeared. [3] Staff and visitors alike are haunted by the empty frames where the stolen works used to be. [4] Today, the <u>museum's</u>
[59]
flourishing programs, concerts, classes, special exhibits, and artist-in-residence are still shadowed by the unsolved mystery, and a reward of millions waits unclaimed.

320. Which option best revises the sentence at the end of paragraph 1?
  (A) No change
  (B) On the night of March 18, 1990, two men dress as police officers demanded entry into the Isabella Stewart Gardener Museum in Boston, Massachusetts, threatened and handcuffed the guards, and made off with 13 works of art valued at over $600 million.
  (C) On the night of March 18, 1990, two men dressed as police officers demanded entry into the Isabella Stewart Gardner Museum in Boston, Massachusetts, threatening the security guards with arrest. They handcuffed him and made off with 13 works of art valued at over $600 million.
  (D) Two men dressed as police officers demanded entry into the Isabella Stewart Gardner Museum in Boston, Massachusetts on the night of March 18, 1990. They threatened the security guards and handcuffed them, then made off with 13 works of art valued at over $600 million.

321.
  (A) No change
  (B) threaten
  (C) threatened
  (D) threats

322. Which option best concludes paragraph 1 and transitions to paragraph 2?

- (A) This museum was the famous art museum built by Isabella Stewart Gardner.
- (B) These stolen pieces were a small, but significant, part of the extensive and priceless collection assembled by Isabella Stewart Gardner during the course of her lifetime.
- (C) Originally owned by Isabela Stewart Gardner, they were now only part of an extensive and priceless collection.
- (D) Though the collection contains over 2,500 items, the ones stolen were favorites of Isabella Stewart Gardner.

323.

- (A) No change
- (B) begins
- (C) has begun
- (D) began

324.

- (A) No change
- (B) treasures; and
- (C) treasure, and
- (D) treasures. and

325.

- (A) No change
- (B) motivated
- (C) convinced
- (D) enabled

326. The author is considering revising the final sentence of paragraph 3. Should the underlined portion be deleted?

- (A) No, because it explains why the stolen art was never replaced
- (B) No, because it explains the stolen art was the only work ever removed
- (C) Yes, because Isabella did not know the art would be stolen when she wrote her will
- (D) Yes, because it talks about adding new works, not replacing what was there

327.

- (A) No change
- (B) it's
- (C) there
- (D) their

328. The author is considering adding the following sentence to paragraph 5. "Some people believe the heist was an inside job organized by one of the security guards, but many are convinced it was organized by the mob." The most logical place would be

(A) after sentence 1.
(B) after sentence 2.
(C) after sentence 3.
(D) after sentence 4.

329.

(A) No change
(B) museums
(C) museums'
(D) museum has

Passage 6

Every new year, I make a resolution to live a healthier life, <u>loose</u> weight, and
330
boost my energy levels. I start off thinking this year is going to be the year <u>it

sticks on me and life changes</u>. Gym memberships, mail order diets, spreadsheets
331
with points and calories and measurements. By February, I'm lucky if I exercise

once a week, and dinner is often takeout, picked up on the way home from work

and mindlessly consumed in front of a television show I rushed home to watch.

The food might <u>have taste</u> good, but I never paid attention. I was too exhausted
332
to think about where it was coming from or what I ordered. Repeated failure

<u>weighed</u> me down, with no solution in sight. Then, one rare day at the gym,
333
I was flipping through *Forbes* magazine, and an article on the top food trends for

the new year caught my eye.

The article stated that the top food trend for the coming year was

mindfulness. Driven by Millennials, mindfulness is a new consumer perspective

<u>of</u> shopping for a product or a brand based on how it aligns with personal
334
values. <u>Understanding, respecting, and valuing the food people put into their

bodies. Thinking about where products come from, how they are produced</u>
335

and distributed, and what impact those choices have on our eating habits. The grocery industry is being pushed to appeal to consumers physically and intellectually, informing and empowering shoppers to make a easier, healthier, [336] and more fun experience. To keep pace with the trends, 17 major food companies have replaced CEOs in the last year in an effort to bring fresh new ideas to the industry.

I knew advertising was designed to make people want to buy products, but it hadn't occurred to me that grocery stores and product brands really studied not only what people were buying, but how and why they were buying it. The article went on to state that 7 out of 10 shoppers want to be able to read and understand the ingredients list, they seek out organic, all-natural, non-GMO [337] labels, and locally sourced products to support their communities. In fact, last year was only the second time since 1900 there was an increase in farmers under the age of 35, suggesting this was a direct result of a shift to mindful eating and shopping.

Although I was curious about the connections to local farming, and what made a product organic or fair-trade certified and why I would want to buy it, I still didn't understand what mindful eating was and how it would benefit me in getting my goals when, thus far, every other diet and exercise plan had failed. [338] How could a diet that lets you eat whatever you want help you lose weight, reduce binge eating and snacking, or increase energy levels? It sounded too good to be true, but mindful eating, often referred to by nutritionists as the anti-diet, is about thinking about every aspect of the food people put in their bodies. What [339] foods do I choose; why am I eating them; how does eating the food make me feel; and where am I eating?

This mind–body connection between food and me was intriguing enough that I started to think about what days I grabbed takeout, how much I would enjoy eating in front of the TV instead of at the table, and how often I overate and felt too full. Becoming more mindful about what food was going into my body and where it came from encouraged healthier, ethically and locally sourced choices that I felt good about physically and emotionally. Changing where I ate meals and how much time I spent eating them renewed my enjoyment of flavors and textures and allowed my brain a healthy amount of time to signal that I was full. In fact, the overall positive influence of mindful eating on my life has resulted in more focus and energy, less stress over dieting and my weight, and increased awareness of my connection to a global community through food.

330.
    (A) No change
    (B) loosing
    (C) losing
    (D) lose

331.
    (A) No change
    (B) life changes, and it sticks on me
    (C) my life changes stick on me.
    (D) it sticks with me, and my life changes

332.
    (A) No change
    (B) have tasted
    (C) taste
    (D) tasted

333.
    (A) No change
    (B) weigh
    (C) weighed
    (D) weighing

334.

    (A) No change
    (B) on
    (C) about
    (D) in

335. Which option would be the most effective revision of the underlined phrases?

    (A) No change
    (B) People should understand, respect, and value the food they put into their bodies. They should think about where products come from, how they are produced and distributed, and the impact of their choices on their eating habits.
    (C) We should understand, respect, and value the food we put into our bodies by thinking about where products comes from, how they are produced and distributed, and the impact those choices have on our eating habits.
    (D) In order to understand, respect, and value the food we put into our bodies, we should think about where products come from, how they are produced and distributed, and the impact of those choices on our eating habits.

336.

    (A) No change
    (B) make easier
    (C) makes an easy
    (D) make an easier

337.

    (A) No change
    (B) list and, they
    (C) list; they
    (D) list; and they

338.

    (A) No change
    (B) achieving
    (C) leaving
    (D) making

339.

    (A) No change
    (B) bodies, what
    (C) bodies: what
    (D) bodies, and what

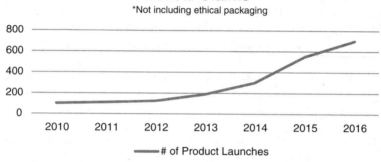

# of Food and Product Launches Featuring Ethical Claims*

*Not including ethical packaging

# of Product Launches

Adapted from information provided by InnovaMarket Insights 2017.

340. Which choice most accurately represents information presented in the graph?

    (A) The number of products featuring ethical claims will continue to rise.
    (B) Companies have increased the number of products featuring ethical claims by almost 300 percent since 2010.
    (C) More products featuring ethical claims are being launched now that Millennials are older and doing their own shopping.
    (D) If consumers stopped buying products based on ethical claims, companies would stop launching them.

341. Information from the graph would be most effective used in which paragraph?

    (A) Paragraph 2
    (B) Paragraph 3
    (C) Paragraph 4
    (D) Paragraph 5

Passage 7

Beginning with George Washington, the United States has had 44 presidents. Donald Trump is considered our 45th president, but Grover Cleveland served two nonconsecutive terms, making the count 44. Each administration had pros and cons. Some were faced with war; some with the expansion of the nation; some with poverty, and many other crises. Others had more <u>quiet</u> experiences.
₃₄₂
Presidents like Lincoln and Kennedy left lasting legacies in the wake of their accomplishments and assassinations. But some presidents were not so impressive and memorable. In fact, despite current social media claims, the most-forgotten "worst presidents ever" were all elected prior to the 1950s. And one of the worst, least memorable <u>was</u> Warren G. Harding, the 29th <u>president from</u> 1921 to 1923.
₃₄₃   ₃₄₄

Warren G. Harding was born in 1865 and grew up in a small town in Ohio with an idyllic American childhood. His parents were doctors, and he had a brother and four sisters. He <u>was attending</u> a one-room school and played
₃₄₅
in the town band. At age 14, Harding enrolled at Ohio Central College and became the editor of the college newspaper and a powerful public speaker. After graduation, Harding took over a local newspaper, *The Marion Daily Star*, and turned it into a very prosperous business. During this time, he met and married a wealthy divorcee, Florence Kling de Wolfe, who encouraged him to enter into politics, more because of his public speaking abilities than any true interest or skills.

[1] His political advancement was due mostly to favors for city bosses, and Harding failed to win the governorship of Ohio on 1910. [2] His bid for US Senate in 1914 was successful, but he was not a very active participant in legislature. [3] As a Republican, he supported business interests and higher tariffs, but even while presenting a strong position, he missed two-thirds of the votes he could have participated in. [4] He was an impressive speaker, had no

major political enemies, and had the "right" stance on all the important issues; these qualities won him the presidential election in 1921.

President Harding's administration was not known for his accomplishments,
347
although there were a few, most notably establishing a budget for the federal government and calling the Washington Naval Disarmament Conference, as well as championing civil liberties for African Americans well before the Civil Rights movement came into existence. Other, less impressive feats included limiting immigration, ending spending controls that had been put in place during wartime, and creating tax cuts for higher incomes. However, Harding was not a very hands-on commander-in-chief and delegated most of the work to his Cabinet members. Three members, Herbert Hoover, Andrew Mellon, and Charles Evans Hughes, were extremely intelligent, capable men who accomplished many things during their time at the White House. Unfortunately, most of Harding's Cabinet, and later his time as president, was labeled with
348
corruption.

The most well-known scandal was the Teapot Dome scandal in which one Cabinet member leased public lands to oil companies in return for personal loans. He was arrested and convicted of taking bribes. Another friend of Harding's was Charles Forbes, director of the Veterans' Bureau, who was caught selling government medical supplies for veterans on the black market. Two other staff members involved with the Veterans' Bureau committed suicide soon after the scandal was known to the public. But the president's own personal scandal
349
did not come to light until after his death.

President Harding died on August 2, 1923, of a heart attack. No autopsy was performed, and some people believe his wife may have poisoned him in order to avoid returning to the White House under the shame of being associated with criminal activities. Later it was discovered he'd had an affair with a woman

named Nan Britton while he was a senator, and DNA identification proved he was the father to her child. 350 Today, these incidents may not seem so <u>shocking and many</u> presidents have faced similar situations and not been judged so harshly. His greatest downfall was his lack of commitment to the responsibilities of being <u>president, that</u> may have made him one of the "worst presidents ever."
                        351

342.

    (A) No change
    (B) uneventful
    (C) positive
    (D) depressing

343.

    (A) No change
    (B) is
    (C) were
    (D) has been

344.

    (A) No change
    (B) president; from
    (C) president, from
    (D) president—from

345.

    (A) No change
    (B) attends
    (C) attended
    (D) had attended

346. The author is considering adding the following sentence to paragraph 3. Which option is the most logical placement for the following sentence: "However, Harding's perspective of the role and responsibilities of a president was more ceremonial than functional."

    (A) After sentence 2
    (B) After sentence 3
    (C) After sentence 4
    (D) Leave it out.

347.

    (A) No change
    (B) their
    (C) its
    (D) it's

348.

    (A) No change
    (B) condemned
    (C) famous
    (D) tainted

349.

    (A) No change
    (B) revealed
    (C) repudiated
    (D) rescinded

350.

    (A) No change
    (B) shocking and, many
    (C) shocking and because
    (D) shocking; many

351.

    (A) No change
    (B) president which
    (C) president that
    (D) president, and

CHAPTER 5

Set 2 Writing and Language Questions

Passage 8

After graduating high school, many young adults are looking for part-time jobs to help pay for college, living expenses, transportation, and social events. However, they need jobs with flexible schedules as their availability could change from semester to <u>semester, they</u> might already
₃₅₂
have another job. The current job market offers many more options for self-employment than ever before. In fact, 10 to 15 percent of the working age population <u>make their living primarily independently</u> employed instead
₃₅₃
of as extra income. The Digital Marketplace, including apps and internet-based businesses, makes up 67 percent of self-employment opportunities. Self-employment is appealing to all ages, education levels, incomes, and occupational interests. You work the hours you want; advancement is dependent on your own motivation; and you can do something you are truly interested in.

[1] One of the most popular and fastest growing careers <u>are</u> driving for a
₃₅₄
rideshare app like Uber or Lyft. [2] Some of the positive reasons people start driving are extra income, working only when they want to, feeling useful,

keeping busy, and meeting new people. [3] The start-up costs to begin driving for Uber or Lyft are very low. [4] Anyone can sign up to begin driving; would-be drivers just need to pass a vehicle inspection because they are required to have a vehicle model newer than 2002 in most states, a background check, and personal car insurance. [5] <u>Before deciding which company to work for, it is important to explore the differences in the hiring process, potential income, the payment</u>
355
<u>process, and both employee and customer satisfaction.</u>

Here are some things to consider about Uber: you can start working independently much sooner than with Lyft. <u>Once you pass the inspections and background check, the training sessions are completed online, and you are</u>
356
<u>ready to go</u>. Lyft pairs new drivers up with veteran drivers for hands-on training throughout the hiring process. It might take longer, but Lyft drivers have reported feeling much more confident and knowledgeable when they begin driving on their own. Drivers reported that Uber is not as <u>accessible</u> as an employer.
357
Communications are mostly in the form of automated email responses, and passenger ratings significantly influence your employment. Lyft also has a ratings system, but passengers go through training when they create a Lyft account, to explain to them how it works, and drivers receive feedback from Lyft based on those ratings. <u>Uber does not.</u>
358
However, you are not going to choose your future employer by its training style or ratings system, but by how much money you can make. Uber drivers tend to be busier than Lyft drivers, but some of this is due to rate cuts for passengers. Uber also takes a 20 percent commission from your rides. Lyft has an incentive-based commission system: the more hours you drive, the lower your commission. Regardless of which company you drive for, you also have to pay out of pocket for gas, insurance, tolls, income taxes, and general vehicle maintenance. Here is an example from an Uber driver who drove 12 hours in

one shift. He made $180, which seems like a decent wage of $15 an hour, but once he subtracted Uber's commission and a percentage for his out-of-pocket expenses, his final profit was only $4.54 per hour.

Both companies have "prime-time hours" and "surge" hours <u>where</u> rates
₃₅₉
increase, and drivers can earn more. But the downside is those hours can be late at night, and passengers might need rides in areas of questionable safety. Full-time drivers say they have had the most success working for both companies, depending on what hours they drive and in what location. Rideshare apps offer a unique opportunity to earn extra income on <u>you're</u> own terms, but as a primary
₃₆₀
source of income, you need to carefully consider all the options of each company and how much time you have available for driving before you make your final decision.

352.

    (A) No change
    (B) semester, and
    (C) semester, yet
    (D) semester, but

353.

    (A) No change
    (B) primarily make their living independently employed
    (C) make their primary living independently employed
    (D) independently make their primary living employed

354.

    (A) No change
    (B) was
    (C) is
    (D) has been

355. The author is considering moving sentence 5 in paragraph 2. Which option is the most logical choice?

    (A) After sentence 1
    (B) After sentence 2
    (C) After sentence 3
    (D) Leave it where it is.

356. Which option improves the flow and clarity of the following sentence in paragraph 3: "Once you pass the inspections and background check, the training sessions are completed online, and you are ready to go"?

(A) You are ready to go once you pass the inspections and the background check, the training sessions are completed online.

(B) The training sessions are completed online, and once you pass the inspections and background check, you are ready to go.

(C) Pass the inspections and the background check, complete the training sessions online, and you are ready to go.

(D) You are ready to go once you pass the inspections, the background check, and the online training sessions.

357.

(A) No change

(B) responsible

(C) personal

(D) accountable

358. Which of the following options would most improve the underlined sentence?

(A) Uber does not talk about the ratings system.

(B) Uber does not have a good ratings system for drivers.

(C) Uber passengers rate drivers, but they do not really understand how the system works.

(D) Uber does not explain the ratings system to passengers or provide feedback to its drivers.

359.

(A) No change

(B) that

(C) when

(D) which

360.

(A) No change

(B) your

(C) they're

(D) their

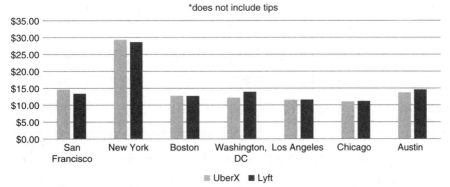

Average Gross Earnings per trip - May 2015

*does not include tips

Adapted from information provided by SherpaShare.

361. Which option most accurately describes the information provided in the graph?

(A) The average amount of money drivers earned in major US cities per hour

(B) The average amount of money drivers earned per trip, before expenses, in major US cities

(C) The average cost of using Uber or Lyft in major US cities

(D) The average amount of money a driver keeps per trip in major US cities

362. The information presented in the graph would most logically go with which paragraph?

(A) Paragraph 1

(B) Paragraph 3

(C) Paragraph 4

(D) Paragraph 5

363. Does the information presented in the graph clearly represent data presented in the passage?

(A) No, because it does not indicate how many drives were averaged, how long the drivers worked, and what the rates were during the hours they drove

(B) Yes, because it shows that drivers earn about the same for both Uber and Lyft, as stated in the passage

(C) No, because it does not take into account the commission or out-of-pocket expenses that drivers must pay for

(D) No, because the passage does not focus on what drivers earn per trip

Passage 9

In every city, in every country, residents and tourists <u>seen</u> the careless vandalism
₃₆₄
of their buildings, walls, and signs. Government officials struggle to identify
culprits who leave gang tags, obscenities, and crude illustrations. The graffiti
<u>promotes</u> a negative vibe and gives neighborhoods, sometimes undeservedly, bad
₃₆₅
reputations. And yet sometimes, seemingly out of nowhere, a piece of art appears
on a canvas of concrete, making a statement loud enough for the world to hear.
One such art "bomber" is an anonymous street artist in London, England,
known only as "Banksy." Banksy is one of the most famous and controversial,
long-lived graffiti artists in the world, producing new works as recently as
January 2018.

Banksy got his start in Bristol, England, in the early 1990s as a teenager,
partnering with other street artists. Even with half a dozen of them, the artwork
took time to create, and it was a close call with the police that finally moved
Banksy to adapt his approach to something that would be faster. <u>His friends all
got to the car and escaped, but Banksy had to hide under a garbage truck for a</u>
₃₆₆
<u>long time, and that was when he decided he needed to be able to complete his
art faster.</u> The idea of using spray paint and precut stencils appealed to him and
became his signature style.

In the early <u>2000s, he</u> headed to London. His art is often full of
₃₆₇
contradictions, dark humor, and satirical perspectives on politics and global
issues. One particular piece of art that represents this is of a young Vietnamese
person who was burned by napalm being escorted by Mickey Mouse and Ronald
McDonald. In 2001, Banksy and a few other street artists had their first "art
opening" in a tunnel on Rivington Street in London. In disguise, they painted
the walls of the tunnel white. Later that week, they held an opening reception,

with hip-hop music blasting and beer from a nearby pub. Nearly 500 people attended. During his last face-to-face interview in 2003 after his "Turf War" exhibition, in response to the debate about maintaining his anonymity, the artist emphasized the importance of a direct connection between the artist and the audience. <u>It wasn't important they know who he is, but that his art is accessible</u>
368
<u>to everyone</u>.

In February 2008, Banksy's work was part of the biggest charity art auction to date, with proceeds totaling $425 million. One of his pieces, titled *Ruined Landscape*, <u>got</u> $385,000; it was a painting of an autumn landscape along a
369
riverbank, with the words "This is not a photo opportunity" stenciled across the middle. Another piece, *A Vandalized Phonebox*, showed an old-fashioned red telephone booth knocked over with a pickax and red paint that looked like blood dripping down the side. This painted was purchased for $605,000.

Banksy continued to challenge authorities and <u>inspired</u> fans, sneaking
370
pieces of his art into famous museums, including the Louvre in France and the Metropolitan Museum of Art in New York City. <u>Critics have called him a</u>
<u>"champagne socialist" he makes millions of dollars and contributes it to various</u>
371
<u>causes, charities, and movements</u>. Today, more than half of his street paintings are only viewable on the internet and are available to download for free. They have been painted over by city workers or worn away by time and weather conditions. Photographs of new art appear on his website, and he challenges fans to find <u>it,</u> sustaining the mystery, the challenge, and the movement that is
372
"Banksy."

364.

    (A) No change
    (B) see
    (C) saw
    (D) have seen

365.

    (A) No change
    (B) resembles
    (C) evokes
    (D) maintains

366. Should the author delete the underlined sentence?

    (A) Yes, because all the relevant information is already stated
    (B) No, because it provides good visual details
    (C) Yes, because the sentence is too long and wordy
    (D) No, because reveals an essential clue to Banksy's identity

367.

    (A) No change
    (B) 2000s—he
    (C) 2000s; he
    (D) 2000s, he

368. The author is considering revising the underlined sentence to improve flow and support the previous statement. Which option best fits that purpose?

    (A) No change
    (B) His identity is not as important as that his art is accessible to everyone.
    (C) The accessibility of his art is more important than revealing his identity.
    (D) Revealing his identity would make his art less important.

369.

    (A) No change
    (B) earned
    (C) raised
    (D) cost

370.

    (A) No change
    (B) inspire
    (C) inspires
    (D) inspiring

371. Which option best corrects the run-on sentence?

(A) No change
(B) Critics have called him, a "<u>champagne socialist</u>," he makes millions of dollars and contributes it to various causes, charities, and movements.
(C) Critics have called him a "champagne socialist" he makes millions of dollars, and contributes it to various causes, charities, and movements.
(D) Critics have called him a "champagne socialist" because he makes millions of dollars and contributes it to various causes, charities, and movements.

372.

(A) No change
(B) him
(C) them
(D) that

373. The following sentence would most logically belong in which paragraph? "His film *Exit Through the Gift Shop* is a controversial documentary about a French immigrant's obsession with street art and was nominated for an Academy Award in 2010."

(A) Paragraph 1
(B) Paragraph 3
(C) Paragraph 4
(D) Paragraph 5

Passage 10

Every second Sunday in March at 2:00 a.m., 48 states in the United States and 72 countries around the world move their clocks from 1:59 a.m. to 3:00 a.m. to begin daylight saving time (DST). DST didn't always <u>exist in fact it only became</u> 374 popular in the last century and a half. Most people believe Benjamin Franklin invented DST. In 1784, he wrote a letter to the *Journal of Paris,* <u>which</u> he was 375 surprised to wake up at 6 a.m. and find the sun up before noon. The letter was considered a joke, and another hundred years or so went by before the idea was brought up again by George Vernon Hudson of New Zealand and a British builder, William Willet. <u>The first suggestion was to turn the clock forward</u>

two hours in October and back two hours in April. <u>New Zealand being in the</u>
<u>southern hemisphere would move the clock opposite of the United States.</u> Later,
₃₇₆
in 1905, Willet suggested a slower change, moving 20 minutes at a time over
four Sundays. Both ideas were rejected.

[1] It wasn't until World War I, when the Germans instituted "war time"
to make better use of daylight hours and conserve <u>energy, that</u> other countries
₃₇₇
also moved the clocks ahead one hour. Thirty-one countries followed their lead
and stopped when the war ended. [2] <u>During World War II, 52 countries used</u>
<u>DST through 1947</u>. [3] President Warren G. Harding hated DST and tried an
₃₇₈
experiment in 1922 where private business didn't have to use DST, even though
the government and Washington, DC, did. [4] The result was disastrous. [5] In
1930, Joseph Stalin forced the former Soviet Union to move the clocks ahead
one hour, and the country forgot to change them back for 61 years.

After the war, some countries and states kept <u>DST, creating</u> chaos and
₃₇₉
confusion. One story states that in 1960 passengers on a bus route from West
Virginia to Ohio had to change their watches seven times! So Congress passed
the Uniform Time Act of 1966, stating that even though states were not required
to use <u>DST</u>, if they did, all states would follow the same guidelines. In 1986,
President Reagan moved the start of DST to the first Sunday in April, and later
the Energy Policy Act of 2005 would move it to precisely 2:00 a.m., the second
Sunday of March, ending 2:00 a.m., the second Sunday of November.

Studies began in the 1970s to determine <u>whether</u> using DST actually saved
₃₈₀
energy. Twenty-five percent of energy goes to electricity, powering lights and
small appliances in homes and businesses. An increase in daylight hours would
reduce this energy use. It also suggests a reduction in traffic accidents during rush
hour, increases in health and moods due to more outdoor activities and exposure
to sunlight, less nighttime crime, and a rise in sales for sporting and recreational
businesses.

There are just as many arguments against DST. The results of the study in 1975 showed only a 1 percent decrease in energy use, and today, <u>society's</u> reliance
₃₈₁
on technology powered by electricity is significantly higher. Other studies suggest that a person's body never really adjusts to the change, and it causes interruptions of the sleep cycles, making <u>them</u> feel tired and affecting the immune system.
₃₈₂
Farmers argue there is no need to change the clocks. They have always adjusted their schedules to increase use of daylight, so business should be able to start earlier instead of relying on a clock change. With no real proof that one way is better than another way, the debate about DST will most likely continue on for some time.

374.

    (A) No change
    (B) exist in fact, it only became
    (C) exist; in fact it only became
    (D) exist, in fact, it only

375.

    (A) No change
    (B) *Journal* in that
    (C) *Journal* that
    (D) *Journal,* which

376. Which option would me the most effective in combining the two sentences for clarity and conciseness?

    (A) The first suggestion was to turn the clocks in New Zealand, in the southern hemisphere, forward two hours in October and back two hours in April, the opposite of the United States.
    (B) The first suggestion was to turn the clocks forward two hours in October and back two hours in April because New Zealand, being in the southern hemisphere, would move the clock opposite to the United States.
    (C) The first suggestion was to turn the clocks forward two hours in October and back two hours in April; New Zealand, being in the southern hemisphere, would move the clock opposite to the United States.
    (D) New Zealand, being in the southern hemisphere, would turn its clock forward two hours in October and back two hours in April was one suggestion.

377.

    (A) No change
    (B) energy, which
    (C) energy that
    (D) energy when

378. The author is considering moving the underlined sentence. Which option is the most logical location?

    (A) No change
    (B) After sentence 3
    (C) After sentence 4
    (D) After sentence 5

379.

    (A) No change
    (B) manifesting
    (C) disseminating
    (D) instigating

380.

    (A) No change
    (B) if
    (C) that
    (D) how

381.

    (A) No change
    (B) societies
    (C) society's
    (D) societys'

382.

    (A) No change
    (B) it
    (C) us
    (D) him or her

383. Which piece of information would be the most useful in supporting the arguments made in paragraph 4?

    (A) Examples of crimes that happen at night
    (B) Statistics showing an increase in profits from sporting and recreational businesses during DST
    (C) The number of small appliances used in households across the United States
    (D) A list of outdoor activities people can do during DST

384. The author is considering revising the final sentence of the passage. Should the author do this?

(A) No, because it has a clever reference to time readers will remember

(B) No, because it reinforces that the use of DST is arbitrary, with no proven benefits or disadvantages

(C) Yes, because it does not summarize all the points made in the essay

(D) Yes, because there is proof of the effect of DST on people's lives

Passage 11

Think about *Harry Potter, Lord of the Rings, Twilight,* and *James Bond.* They are all blockbuster movies originally based on books. Tom Clancy's character Jack Ryan <u>appearing</u> in movies for over three decades beginning with *The Hunt for*
385
Red October and more recently *Jack Ryan: Shadow Recruit.* Audiences today, according to surveys, are much more likely to go see a movie that is "based on" <u>something—a novel</u>, series, or true-life event. The process of turning a book into
386
a movie is a long and very unpredictable one. There are many things to think about before a script is written from a book or a book is even selected. Most times it is not even the authors who <u>tries</u> to get their books turned into films.
387

[1] The first step in turning a book into film is to pick the right book. [2] Not all books make good films. [3] The plot might not offer enough suspense to keep an audience interested or the scope of the novel might be too complex to <u>put in to</u>
388
a two-hour movie. [4] <u>The material too obscure or too common.</u> [5] Usually
389
bestselling books or plots with unusual twists are chosen for movies, which isn't to say other books would not make good TV movies or series. [6] No matter what, there <u>are</u> always risks when going to make "the pitch." [7] The pitch is
390
when a proposal to make a book into a movie is sent out to producers, hoping someone will be interested. [8] Most successful writers already have contacts through their literary agents or publishing companies, but it is important to have a successful introduction to the movie world when making the pitch.

Once a director decides he or she likes the concept of the book, they agree to options. The option is payment to the author for considering the book. <u>The option is not a guarantee the book will be made into a movie, but it is a contract with very certain guidelines for what happens if the movie is made and release</u>
391
<u>about everything from what the author earns all the way through how many free tickets the author gets to the movie premier.</u> It could include a deadline for consideration, whether the author will be included in the credits, and whether the author will get to review the script. The final step for a book to be turned into a movie is writing the script. <u>The author is rarely involved in this part because it is a totally different kind of writing, and it is important to find the</u>
392
<u>right director for the vision of the film and give artistic freedom to interpret the book in the best way possible for the movie.</u>

Stephen King has had more books turned into films than any other writer. When he enters into an option with a producer, he asks for a dollar; approvals over the screenwriter, director, and principal cast; and a share in whatever profits come in. King states in an interview that he has not always liked the film versions of his book, but directors who are persistent and edgy get his attention. Stanley Kubrick's *The Shining* "wasn't what he imagined." The movie <u>oversimplified in his opinion </u>the emotional struggles of the characters, and he
393
doesn't take credit for successes or failures because he doesn't make the movies.

[1] Not all authors can distance themselves that way. [2] Stephanie Meyers, author of the *Twilight* series, struggles with criticism of her book because of the way things are portrayed in the movie, even though she had very little to do with writing the script. [3] Her success with *Twilight* has labeled her a fantasy writer, so no one is interested in reading her other, non-fantasy, books. [4] It's possible a bad movie can <u>make the book look bad</u> or disappoint the audience when the
394
only thing the book and movie have in common is the title. [5] Some books,

like *Gone with the Wind, The Godfather, The Shining, Lord of the Rings*, and *Harry Potter*, have become some of the greatest movies of all time, and cultural icons whose popularity will never fade.

385.
    (A) No change
    (B) appears
    (C) appeared
    (D) appear

386.
    (A) No change
    (B) something, a novel
    (C) something: a novel
    (D) something a novel

387.
    (A) No change
    (B) tried
    (C) trying
    (D) try

388.
    (A) No change
    (B) make
    (C) include
    (D) sustain

389. The author wants to combine the underlined phrase with another sentence. Which option is the most logical choice?
    (A) Sentence 2
    (B) Sentence 3
    (C) Sentence 5
    (D) Sentence 6

390.
    (A) No change
    (B) is
    (C) was
    (D) were

391. The author is considering revising the underlined sentence Which option is the most logical choice to improve clarity and conciseness?

(A) No change

(B) The option is not a guarantee the book will be made into a movie, but it is a contract with very certain guidelines for what happens if the movie is made and released, what the author earns, and how many free tickets the author gets to the movie premier.

(C) The option is a contract with specific guidelines for what happens if the movie is made and released, including what the author earns and how many free tickets the author receives for the premier.

(D) The option does not guarantee the book will be made into a movie, but if it is, all the details are specifically outlined in the contract.

392. The author is considering deleting this sentence. Would this improve the flow and focus of the paragraph?

(A) No, because it is important information about screenwriting

(B) No, because someone might assume the author writes the movie script

(C) Yes, because it does not relate to the last step in turning the book into a movie

(D) Yes, because the information presents a new topic not previously mentioned in the paragraph

393.

(A) No change

(B) simplified, in his opinion,

(C) simplified in his opinion,

(D) simplified; in his opinion,

394.

(A) No change

(B) have a negative influence

(C) impact readers' opinions of a book

(D) ruin a book

395. The author wants to include the following sentence in the final paragraph, "They struggle with many factors outside of their control once their books are made into films." Which is the most logical place to insert the sentence?

(A) After sentence 1

(B) After sentence 2

(C) After sentence 3

(D) After sentence 4

Passage 12

The term *alien invaders* often <u>conjure</u> up colorful images of flying saucers or
         396
giant robots from outer space trying to wipe out humanity. It does not usually

make a person think of fish. But the Asian carp is an invader. This fish is just one

of hundreds of species that do not belong in America's ecosystem, and now

that <u>their</u> here, they aren't going anywhere. The fish were originally brought to
      397
the United States in the 1980s by various fish farmers as a natural alternative to

clean artificially created ponds in Arkansas and other Southern and Midwestern

states along the Mississippi River. When massive flooding occurred in the 1990s,

those fish were able to escape the self-contained farm ponds into the rivers,

jumping as high as four feet out of the water, and as they traveled north, they

consumed everything in their path.

[1] Many people wonder why a fish could be so dangerous. [2] There are four

species of Asian carp currently breeding in American waterways. The silver carp

can grow up to 70 pounds and lay hundreds of thousands of eggs at one time.

[3] That is a lot of mouths to feed. Because the carp are filter feeders, meaning

they strain small plankton and nutrients from the bottoms of rivers and lakes,

they are <u>taking</u> enormous amounts of food that would usually feed the smaller
       398
native fish. [4] Native fish, like the walleye, are smaller and fewer. [5] Their eggs

are small enough to be accidentally eaten by large carp. [6] And the aggressive

behaviors of the carp are also killing off more fragile species like zebra and

quagga mussels and the round goby fish living in the Great Lakes.

The Great Lakes are an area of concern when it comes to the voracious

appetites of the Asian carp. The fishing industry there is currently valued at $7

billion a year. It is not just fishermen who are concerned; local mayors and state

governments are also investing in research and technologies aimed at stopping this threat to the economy and the fragile Great Lakes ecosystem. Illinois and the federal government have spent $400 million over the years trying to keep

400

these fish away from the Great Lakes. To stop the spread of the carp, there is an underwater electrical barrier on the Chicago Sanitary and Ship Canal. There are three electrical barriers currently operating along the river where the carp are most likely expected to travel north. The National Park Service and Michigan's Department of Natural Resources are testing new barriers and higher dams the fish could not jump over. 401

The Aquatic Nuisance Species Task Force encourages and supports "active control" of the fish. In some areas this means holding fishing contests for the carp. The carp is actually a delicious fish and offers an abundant and nutritious source of food for people so local restaurants are encouraged to have it on their

402

menus to promote demand for the fish, in hopes of reducing the population. Continued research and control methods are also being studied and tested. The Asian Carp Regional Coordinating Committee does DNA monitoring on the fish. Samplings using electrofishing help determine the numbers of fish present in a given area and provide a forensic map of where a fish was swimming over the course of it's lifetime. This information is put into a database to track where

403

fish are coming from and how far they might travel.

Not everyone is as concerned that the carp could take over the Great Lakes should the barriers fail. There are currently at least 100 invasive species present in the lakes, disrupting the native species, and to date, less than a dozen Asian carp have made it through all the barriers to get within 10 miles of Lake Michigan. Reverting the Mississippi River back to its original flow might only result in endangering the ecosystems of 31 other states whose waterways are all connected. Lake scientists say Lakes Michigan, Huron, and Superior are in no danger even if a few carp get in, because the lakes could not hold a breeding population. First,

404

a closed lake system would not produce enough food for the fish to grow to a massive size, and second, the carp must lay their eggs in moving water. In spite of the debates on the actual danger of the invasion, how much money to invest, and how to study these fish, the one thing everyone can agree on is that Asian carp are here to stay.

396.

    (A) No change
    (B) conjures
    (C) conjure
    (D) does conjure

397.

    (A) No change
    (B) they're
    (C) its
    (D) it's

398.

    (A) No change
    (B) destroying
    (C) consuming
    (D) contaminating

399. The author would like to add the following sentence to paragraph 2. "The fish are also dangerous to humans, jumping out of the water with an impact force strong enough to knock a person out of a boat or unconscious." Which location is the most logical choice?

    (A) After sentence 2
    (B) After sentence 3
    (C) Before sentence 5
    (D) Before sentence 6

400.

    (A) No change
    (B) has spent
    (C) had spent
    (D) spent

401. The author is considering adding a new final sentence to paragraph 3. Which option makes the most sense?

(A) No change

(B) If the fishing industry truly wants to protect itself, it needs to start helping the government pay for the research and development of these systems.

(C) However, there is no proof any of this will work, and millions of dollars could be wasted.

(D) To date, these methods seem to be working, although they are not foolproof.

402.

(A) No change

(B) people, but

(C) people. Local

(D) people, so

403.

(A) No change

(B) its

(C) their

(D) there

404.

(A) No change

(B) increase

(C) decrease

(D) sustain

Total Expenditures on Asian Carp Activities in 2015			
National Agency	**Total Amount**	**Individual States**	**Total Amount**
USACE	$28,542,985.00	Indiana	$421,001.00
USDA Forest Service	$27,000.00	Iowa	$146,378.00
USGS	$8,238,472.00	Kentuckey	$130,000.00
NOAA	$44,220.00	Illinois	$4,357,000.00
USFWS	$4,673,533.00	Minnesota	$1,910,011.00
USCG 9th Divison	$46,648.00	Missouri	$119,929.00
NPS	$40,000.00	Ohio	$1,041,038.00
		Pennsylvania	$40,000.00
		Tennessee	$78,000.00
Totals	$41,612,858.00		$8,243,357.00

405. According to the graph and supported by the passage, which states are most at risk for the invasion of Asian carp into their waterways?

    (A) States that touch the Great Lakes

    (B) States along the Mississippi River

    (C) Illinois

    (D) All the states in the Mississippi River Basin region

406. The United States Army Corps of Engineers spent over $28 million to design and build barriers against the Asian carp in 2015. This information would be best used as supporting evidence in which paragraph?

    (A) Paragraph 1

    (B) Paragraph 2

    (C) Paragraph 3

    (D) Paragraph 4

407. Based on the information presented in the graph, the author would most likely agree with which of the following statements?

    (A) States need to invest more money into protections instead of asking the federal government for funds.

    (B) Too much money has been spent on barriers that don't work.

    (C) The Asian carp is an expensive problem that requires states and federal agencies to collaborate more efficiently.

    (D) States will go broke trying to stop an inevitable takeover by the carp.

Passage 13

Every year, on November 8th, the Aymara people celebrate Bolivia's *Día de las Ñatitas*, the Day of the Skulls. The Aymara are one of 11 tribes related to South
<u>408</u>
America, specifically in Peru and Bolivia, that predate the Incan Empire. The Aymara <u>has</u> slowly migrated toward the larger, more established cities, bringing
409
their heritage and traditions with them. *Ñatitas*, which translates to something like "little pug-nosed ones," refers to the skulls, which are the guests of honor during this special festival.

    [1] These skulls live in places of honor in the homes of the Aymara people. [2] Most families have small shrines or beautifully decorated cases for them. [3] These skulls could be from deceased relatives, passed down from generation to

generation as family heirlooms, or dug up from an unknown grave and given a new life as a *ñatita*. [4] The Aymara believe humans have seven souls. [5] When a person dies, six of those souls go to heaven or the <u>after life and</u> one stays inside
410
the skull. [6] The skulls, which are associated with fertility, luck, and protection, then grant blessings to the home and family of their caretaker. [7] But not every skull makes a good *ñatita*. [8] If the personalities of the skull and its owner conflict, the person could be cursed by the skull with illness, misfortune, or financial loss. [9] When a skull is purchased from a grave robber instead of being dug up honorably, this can happen.

The festival begins in the home, where skulls are brought out <u>in hats,</u>
<u>sunglasses, jewelry, and other accessories.</u> and elaborately dressed and decorated
412
for the occasion. Fresh flowers and cocoa leaves are offered to each skull, but to make it happy, it is essential to have cigarettes, alcohol, and live music. When the skulls are happy, the family may ask them for blessings. These could include protection, cures for illness, helping a child with homework, or financial success. Even police officers have *ñatitas* and swear they help solve cases and catch murderers. Once the skulls are prepared, they are paraded through the streets to the central church in La Paz for a blessing.

The relationship between the Catholic Church and the Aymara people is a
<u>fragile</u> one. When the Spanish conquest began in 1535, the indigenous people
413
were harshly punished for practicing their ancient traditions, including having *ñatitas*. For two centuries, they practiced their beliefs in secret from the Church, until a rebellion in 1780. For a while, the Church <u>refusing</u> to bless the skulls but
414
did not actively punish practitioners, until 2003, when the refusal resulted in rocks being thrown at the church, smashing the windows. Although the Church still will not perform a mass, they will bless the skulls and sprinkle holy water

on them as they parade through the aisles. Once the ceremony is complete, the skulls are escorted to the large central cemetery and displayed for the rest of the day.

An average of 10,000 people join the festivities at the cemetery, bringing their own skulls or asking blessings of the skulls that are present year after year. Some skulls are famous, showing up year after year and bringing good fortune to their owners and anyone who asks for protection and a blessing. <u>And of course, what is a good festival without a night of epic parties to follow?</u> Every year, hundreds
₄₁₅
of people <u>sing, dance, and celebrate</u> long into the night to honor the *ñatitas*
₄₁₆
as full-fledged participants in their lives, not as macabre reminders of a dead person. The Day of the Skulls <u>are</u> not about the person who died, but about the
₄₁₇
spirit of the skull that lives on. In Bolivia, "the dead are only as dead as you allow them to be."

408.

    (A) No change
    (B) indigenous
    (C) alien
    (D) invasive

409.

    (A) No change
    (B) had
    (C) have
    (D) delete completely

410.

    (A) No change
    (B) afterlife; and
    (C) afterlife, and
    (D) afterlife and,

411. The author is considering adding the following sentence, "After a body has 'rested' for a while after its death, the skulls should be dug up and cared for to appease the remaining spirit." Which is the most logical placement in paragraph 2?

(A) After sentence 3
(B) After sentence 4
(C) After sentence 5
(D) After sentence 6

412. The author is considering moving the underlined phrase. Which option is the most logical choice?

(A) Leave it where it is.
(B) After the word *dressed*
(C) After the word *decorated*
(D) After the word *occasion*

413.

(A) No change
(B) volatile
(C) sympathetic
(D) symbiotic

414.

(A) No change
(B) refused
(C) refuses
(C) refuse

415. The author is considering deleting the underlined sentence. Would this make sense?

(A) No, because the next sentence talks about parties
(B) Yes, because the next sentence gives enough information about the celebrations
(C) No, because it makes the reader feel included in the passage
(D) Yes, because the tone does not match the rest of the passage

416.

(A) No change
(B) singing, dancing, and celebrating
(C) sang, danced, and celebrated
(D) have sung, danced, and celebrated

417.

    (A) No change

    (B) was

    (C) is

    (D) were

Passage 14

Route 66 is the <u>epitome</u> of the Great American Road Trip. It's "two thousand
₄₁₈
miles all the way," according to Nat King Cole in his famous song, "Get Your

Kicks on Route 66." The song may not offer much information about what to do

when you get there, but it is a good starting place if you want to take a drive and

experience the history of Americana. <u>Considered the "Main Street of America"</u>
₄₁₉
Route 66 winds from Chicago, Illinois, all the way to Los Angeles, California

(or Santa Monica depending on how true to the route you stay). It began life

as part of the National Old Trails Highway, and once it was <u>paved, in 1926, it</u>
₄₂₀
became more than just a road. It became a lifeline to small towns across the Mid

and Southwest regions of the United States, and now it is one of the most popular

road trips to take in America, with dozens of attractions to see in every state.

Not <u>anyone</u> has two to three weeks or more to experience the entire trip, but
₄₂₁
for a taste of the true Route 66, the 401 miles crossing through Arizona will

more than satisfy the yearnings of any wanderer. Arizona is home to some of the

longest stretches of the original highway still in existence. 422 This is mostly due

to the <u>"Angel of the Mother Road" a man named Angel Delgadillo</u> born and

raised right on the side of the original Route 66 highway in Seligman, Arizona.

The "Mother Road" is a reference to John Steinbeck's novel, *The Grapes of Wrath*,

and Delgadillo <u>think</u> it fits Route 66, which gave birth to numerous small towns
₄₂₃
and businesses. He witnessed some of the most important events <u>on</u> our history
₄₂₄
travel right in front of his barbershop, like families escaping the Dust Bowl and

abandoning farms during the Great Depression, and supplies being brought West during World War II.

It all changed on September 22, 1978, when Interstate 40 opened, bypassing Seligman and dozens of other small towns in favor of high-speed travel between large cities and major attractions. Slowly businesses died down or closed. Towns began to empty out. Families had no money coming in to support them.
425
Delgadillo decided to take a stand to save his home and the historic entity that is Route 66. In 1987, he convinced many business owners to create the Historic Route 66 Association of Arizona. They were able to preserve a 159-mile stretch of the road, with only small pieces no longer accessible, and slowly start to resurrect that nostalgic feeling that visitors were coming to experience. Seligman, Arizona, is just one town that brings in tourists from all over the world.
426
Arizona is also the home of several other unique attractions along Route 66. For example, the famous Wigwam Village Motel in Holbrook has been in existence since the 1930s, and travelers can still book nights to sleep in large, individual rooms that resemble Native American structures. The Blue Swallow Motel is also still in operation and famous for it's colorful vintage neon signs. There are many ways to spend time in this off-the-beaten-path town. Classic
427
diners, vintage cafés, and shops full of interesting souvenirs like the Rainbow Rock Shop with its collection of dinosaurs outside.

[1] In addition to the museums, gift shops, and restaurants, Arizona also has some of the most stunning natural landscapes along the entire route. [2] The Painted Desert stretches from the southeastern corner of the Grand Canyon to the Petrified Forest National Park. [3] The landscapes are a rainbow of colors, from oranges to reds, blues, pinks, golds, and browns. [4] The Petrified Forest is made up of the leftovers of a pine forest buried by ash and silica from an ancient
428
volcanic eruption, and it hardened over time into a rock-like material. [5] Wind

and water erosion have slowly revealed the skeletons of these ancient trees. East of the Grand Canyon sits Meteor Crater. Sixty stories deep and 20 football fields across, the crater dates back 50,000 years and is the best-preserved impact site on Earth. [6] No matter what inspires the journey, the experience of a trip down Route 66 preserves a history of America that <u>would</u> otherwise be forgotten.
₄₂₉

418.

    (A) No change
    (B) icon
    (C) symbol
    (D) superstar

419. The author is considering deleting the underlined words. Does this make sense?

    (A) No, because it gives the nickname of the road
    (B) No, because people know Main Street means the most important street in a town
    (C) Yes, because it is unnecessary information
    (D) Yes, because the sentence does not explain the nickname

420.

    (A) No change
    (B) paved; in 1926, it
    (C) paved in 1926; it
    (D) paved in 1926, it

421.

    (A) No change
    (B) someone
    (C) everyone
    (D) no one

422.

    (A) No change
    (B) "Angel of the Mother Road" a man, named Angel Delgadillo,
    (C) "Angel of the Mother Road," a man named Angel Delgadillo,
    (D) "Angel of the Mother Road." A man named Angel Delgadillo

423.

    (A) No change
    (B) was thinking
    (C) thought
    (D) thinks

424.

    (A) No change
    (B) in
    (C) of
    (D) about

425. Which option best combines the two sentences?

    (A) Towns began to empty out, and families had no money coming in to support them.
    (B) Towns began to empty out because families had no money coming in to support them.
    (C) Towns began to empty out, but families had no money coming in to support them.
    (D) Towns began to empty out then families had no money to coming in to support them.

426. The author does not feel the underlined sentence makes a strong conclusion for paragraph 4. Which option provides the most logical place to move to the sentence?

    (A) The first sentence of paragraph 5
    (B) The last sentence of paragraph 3
    (C) The first sentence of paragraph 4
    (D) Leave it where it is.

427.

    (A) No change
    (B) town: classic
    (C) town, classic
    (D) town—classic

428.

    (A) No change
    (B) remnants
    (C) casualties
    (D) decomposition

429.

    (A) No change
    (B) will
    (C) won't
    (D) can't

430. The author is considering adding another paragraph. Which topic makes the most sense to include in the passage?

    (A) A paragraph about the costs of the road trip
    (B) A paragraph about the Grand Canyon
    (C) A paragraph about Arizona's Native American tribes
    (D) A paragraph about Angel Delgadillo's family

CHAPTER 6

Set 3 Writing and Language Questions

Passage 15

Everyone has heard of Walt Disney, but some people do not know it is actually the name of the man behind the mouse—Mickey Mouse. The man, Walter Elias Disney, was born in Hermosa, Illinois, on December 5, 1901. <u>He came from a very typical upbringing.</u> Disney grew up in Missouri
431
with his four siblings. He loved trains <u>and as he got older</u> would spend
432
his summers working on the trains, selling snacks to travelers. At a young age, he was encouraged in his drawing by an aunt and a neighbor. He took photography and drawing in high school, but his family <u>moves</u> a lot for his
433
father to find work, so school never really interested Disney.

He dropped out of high school at age 16 with the intention of joining the army during World War I. He was rejected due to his young age; instead, Disney traveled to France and volunteered for the Red Cross, driving an ambulance. A year later, in 1919, he returned to the United States and began looking for a job as a newspaper artist. His first professional job was for KC Film Advertising Company, doing hand-drawn cel animation, in which each frame is drawn by hand and then put together to be filmed at a high speed so the frames look seamless. Disney used this experience to open his own studio, producing short, animated cartoons called <u>Laugh-o-grams, but</u>

<u>434</u>

declared bankruptcy in 1923.

    <u>This did not get Walt Disney down.</u> Moving to California with his brother,

435

they went to work for Iwerks Studio and soon produced the first Mickey Mouse

cartoons. <u>These</u> were not as popular as Disney had hoped, but finally, when

436

sound could be combined with the animation, he had a hit with *Steamboat*

Willie, using his very own voice for Mickey Mouse from 1928 through 1947. In

1932, he won his first Academy Award for the short subject cartoon category,

and then again for the next seven years. *Snow White and the Seven Dwarfs* was

the first full-length, animated feature film and received a total of eight Academy

Awards. Overall, Disney still holds the record for most individual Oscar wins,

with 33, and nominations, with 59.

    [1] During World War II, Disney struggled to keep his new Burbank,

California, studio open amidst strikes by his employees. [2] He focused on

compilations of short cartoons and made propaganda films for the United States.

[3] <u>At the beginning</u> of the war, Disney did not want to taint the reputation

437

of his studio with obviously propagandist works, but eventually his studio

did produce anti-Nazi cartoons and other animated shorts using the character

of Donald Duck. [4] Disney Studios produced over 400,000 feet of film for

US military training, war support, and patriotic films. [5] This is equal to 68

hours of viewing time. [6] <u>Some of these films were part of "The New Spirit"</u>

438

<u>campaign encouraging citizens to pay their taxes to support the war.</u>

    After the war was over, Walt Disney returned to feature-length animated

films, and in the next decade, he produced six more movies: *Cinderella, Treasure*

Island, Alice in Wonderland, Lady and the Tramp, Peter Pan, and *101 Dalmatians*.

His Burbank studio produced over 100 films. In addition to film production,

Disney designed and <u>open</u> his first amusement park, Disneyland, in California

439

in 1955. Although he passed away in 1966, his brother, Roy Disney, went on to carry out his brother's dream and opened Walt Disney World in Orlando, Florida, in 1971. Today, with Disney parks in countries around the world, movies, merchandise, television networks, and billions of dollars in revenue each year, it is easy to forget <u>the legacy the man leaves behind as a groundbreaking filmmaker whose contributions changed animated film production forever</u>. His
own words—"dream, create, inspire"—are still used today, in every park, with all employees, to remind them what the true spirit of Disney is.

431. The author is considering deleting the underlined sentence. Which is the best option?

(A) Yes, because it does not offer any relevant details

(B) Yes, because his childhood is mentioned in the rest of the paragraph

(C) No, because people need to know his childhood was typical

(D) No, because it helps explain the rest of the paragraph

432.

(A) No change

(B) and, as he got older, would

(C) and; as he got older would

(D) and as he got older; would

433.

(A) No change

(B) does move

(C) will move

(D) moved

434.

(A) No change

(B) Laugh-o-grams; but

(C) Laugh-o-grams but

(D) Laugh-o-grams—but

435.

(A) No change

(B) This did not bring Walt Disney down.

(C) This did not discourage Walt Disney.

(D) This did not get Walt Disney discouraged.

436.

    (A) No change
    (B) they
    (C) those
    (D) them

437.

    (A) No change
    (B) in the beginning
    (C) about the beginning
    (D) around the beginning

438. Should the author relocate the underlined sentence?

    (A) Leave it where it is.
    (B) Yes, after sentence 2
    (C) Yes, after sentence 3
    (D) Yes, after sentence 4

439.

    (A) No change
    (B) opened
    (C) opens
    (D) opening

440. Which option best revised the underlined portion of the sentence?

    (A) No change
    (B) the legacy of a groundbreaking filmmaker who changed animated film production forever
    (C) the legacy of the man who was a groundbreaking filmmaker and changed animated film production forever
    (D) the legacy that changed animated film production forever by a groundbreaking man

Passage 16

Over the last three or four decades, there has been a big push for high school graduates to go to college for academic degrees. Schools are putting more focus on academic preparation for higher education, but it isn't always the best fit
₄₄₁
for everyone. Students have less exposure to hands-on training unless they attend a technical school, and this has resulted in a significant decrease in the

number of young people entering into vocational fields. For the past several years, skilled trades have been listed as the hardest positions to fill when hiring new employees. Skilled trades <u>refers</u> to any occupation that requires specialized,
442
hand-on skills; skilled trade people include machinists, welders, electricians, plumbers, mechanical engineers, and large machine operators.

[1] After the recession in 2008–2009, hundreds if not thousands of skilled trade people were out of work. [2] The housing market <u>crashed and</u> no new
443
construction was happening. [3] These workers often left the trade for other careers to put money in their pockets and food on their tables. [4] But as the economy improves, the demand for these trades is increasing, and those workers are now significantly older. [5] Approximately 53 percent of trade workers are over the age of 45. For electricians, this number is 60 percent. [6] Estimates indicate 3 million jobs could open up in the next decade, but at current hiring rates, two-thirds of those would <u>be</u> unfilled.
445
The vocational trades have a bad reputation as jobs for uneducated or unskilled laborers, for being low-paying or lacking in advancement opportunities. But <u>all</u> of this is untrue. Most trades require a very specialized
446
set of skills. Manufacturing, for example, no longer pertains to assembly lines of workers putting items together, but to someone with the technology and problem-solving skills to program, maintain, and repair the equipment. It offers opportunities for advancement and good starting wages, and when combined with relevant further education, can offer career paths that earn large salaries.

Plumbing is another example of an evolving, high-demand trade. Whether it is new construction, rebuilding from natural disasters, or unclogging the pipes under the sink, plumbers are needed ubiquitously. But plumbing isn't just pipes anymore; it's using green technology, harvesting rainwater, and sanitizing water for hurricane victims, among other things. <u>Construction workers need to be</u>

<u>highly intelligent with good math skills and excellent spatial abilities, in addition</u>
447
<u>to having good interpersonal and problem-solving skills.</u> According to the

US Census Bureau, people who have four-year degrees, excluding those who go

on to graduate school, in humanities <u>has</u> the lowest earnings because they are
448
much less likely to be working in their fields of study.

This isn't to say that high school students should abandon college degrees in

favor of becoming a welder or wind turbine engineer, but the Bureau of Labor

Statistics does report that many careers that don't require four-year degrees have

average starting salaries above $40,000 a year. Most of these trades would give

someone the opportunity to start working and earning immediately, often with

on-the-job training, in a field that interests them. Workers could then elect to

move on to higher education that <u>relates to</u> advancing in their fields while not
449
accruing significant debt. In many cases, employers will pay for the coursework

or training as an incentive.

441. Should the author delete the underlined sentence?
- (A) Yes, because it repeats information previously implied
- (B) Yes, because it places the blame on the schools for students' choices
- (C) No, because it specifies what the schools are focusing on
- (D) No, it should replace the first sentence.

442.
- (A) No change
- (B) referred
- (C) referring
- (D) refer

443.
- (A) No change
- (B) crashed and,
- (C) crashed, and
- (D) crashed; and

444. Which location in paragraph 2 would be the best fit for the following sentence? "Trades people rarely work past the earliest retirement age because the work can be very physically demanding, and when these workers retire, it could mean serious problems for the United States manufacturing and construction industries."

- (A) After sentence 1
- (B) After sentence 3
- (C) After sentence 5
- (D) After sentence 6

445.

- (A) No change
- (B) remain
- (C) become
- (D) go

446.

- (A) No change
- (B) most
- (C) some
- (D) none

447. The author is considering moving or deleting the underlined sentence. Which option makes the most sense to maintain the flow and focus of the passage?

- (A) Move it to paragraph 3, which talks about the skills of the workers.
- (B) Leave it where it is.
- (C) Delete it because the passage does not talk about construction workers at all.
- (D) Move it to the final paragraph, which talks about gaining advanced education and skills.

448.

- (A) No change
- (B) had
- (C) make
- (D) got

449.

- (A) No change
- (B) results in
- (C) corresponds with
- (D) invests in

450. The author feels the final sentence may not provide a strong conclusion to the passage. Which option best fits as a concluding sentence?

(A) No change

(B) If more people don't start working in trades, society is going to have a lot of problems maintaining buildings.

(C) Providing this information to young people might interest them in vocational work and ensure a solid future for these vital services.

(D) If young people knew that working in trades could help them pay for college, most of them would want to learn these skills.

Passage 17

It is very common when a child is born for family and friends to comment on the features of the baby—mom's nose, dad's chin, or grandpa's ears. They will speculate about eye color, hair color, and height. As the child grows up, maybe he or she has an outgoing personality like grandma, or dad's sense of humor. These traits are no accident. Every person has expressed traits, like physical appearance, and inherent traits like personality or health. These traits come from genes passed down by the parents. A child receives one set from each <u>parent, and</u>
                                                                          451
depending on the combinations of dominant and recessive genes, these traits will manifest themselves in different ways, sometimes immediately and sometimes later on in life.

Dominant <u>meant</u> that particular trait will be manifested by the person,
         452
and <u>only one parent is needed</u>. Recessive genes need two genes, one from each
    453
parent, in order to be expressed. For example, brown hair is a dominant gene, and red hair is recessive. Usually, the child will have brown hair, unless both parents carry a recessive red hair gene. The concept of inherited dominant and recessive traits <u>were</u> first discovered in 1854 by Gregor Mendel, an Austrian
                        454
monk. In his experiments using pea plants, he was able to trace how traits from parent plants were passed on to new plants. This discovery of how some traits were passed on randomly and some traits followed statistical probabilities of

appearance directly countered previous beliefs that all traits were a result of the
parents traits blended together equally.
        455

Mendel's research led to the discovery of different kinds of dominance in
genes. In addition to complete dominance, when only the dominant trait is
visible, there is incomplete dominance, which occurs when traits merge together
to form a completely new trait. When a red flower and a white flower are cross-
                                              456
pollinated to make a pink flower. If the red flower and white flower result in
a white flower with red splotches, it is codominance. In both of these cases,
though, neither parent could have recessive genes. Looking at physical traits is
the most obvious way to study the results of combining dominant and recessive
genes, but a more important application would be determining the health factors
inherited from parents.

  Genetic disorders result from defective genes that have abnormal function
                                        457
that produce too much or too little of something in the body. People can be
unaffected, meaning they do not carry the gene. Affected means a person
inherited two copies of the defective gene and displays the disorder. Or a person
can be a carrier with one defective gene that is not displayed because of other
dominant genes. Some examples of genetic disorders linked to recessive genes are
cystic fibrosis, sickle cell anemia, and Tay Sachs disease. Multifactoral diseases are
caused by a combination of genes and environmental factors: heart disease, most
cancers, diabetes, alcoholism, obesity, and Alzheimer's disease. Chromosomal
disorders like Down syndrome result from an excess or deficiency of a gene.

  Modern science and DNA testing can reveal a lot about genetics and genetic
disorders. The ability to test embryos for genetic disorders and diseases is causing
many ethical dilemmas for doctors and parents. Couples, in most cases ones who
                              458
struggle with pregnancy, have the option to test embryos for specific disorders,
and depending on the results, they have to determine if they are willing to live

with the risks of following through with the pregnancy. In some cases, parents may decide they are willing to face whatever challenges they may face. In other situations, if the disorder is known to be very serious and have a high mortality rate, the parents may decide not to follow through with the pregnancy.

The science of genetics is a complex one. People can look in a mirror and see mom's eyes, dad's hair, and Great Aunt Lucy's blue eyes, or hear the same laugh as their siblings or have a cousin's similar lack of coordination. But they can't see what is on the inside, and with environmental factors having more impact now than ever before, the research that is being done could improve a lot of lives and prevent many diseases.

451.

    (A) No change
    (B) parent, and,
    (C) parent and,
    (D) parent and

452.

    (A) No change
    (B) meaning
    (C) means
    (D) mean

453. The author is considering revising the underlined phrase for clarity. Which option provides the most clarity?

    (A) No change
    (B) only one parent is needed to give the gene
    (C) only one from the dominant parent is needed
    (D) only one dominant gene from the parent is needed.

454.

    (A) No change
    (B) had been
    (C) would be
    (D) was

455.

(A) No change
(B) parent's traits
(C) parents' traits
(D) parents trait's

456.

(A) No change
(B) trait when
(C) trait, when
(D) trait; when

457. Which option most clearly and concisely revises the underlined sentence?

(A) No change
(B) Genetic disorders result from defective genes in the body that produce too much or too little of something and function abnormally.
(C) Genetic disorders result from defective genes functioning abnormally to produce too much or too little of something in the body.
(D) Genetic disorders result from defective genes producing too much or too little of something in the body.

458.

(A) No change
(B) from
(C) with
(D) between

		Parent #1	Blue eyes
		b	**b**
B	Parent #2	Bb	Bb
b	Brown eyes	bb	bb

459. According to the Punnit square, what is the probability this child will have brown eyes?

(A) 25 percent
(B) 50 percent
(C) 75 percent
(D) 100 percent

460. What is the probability this child will have blue eyes?

(A) 25 percent
(B) 50 percent
(C) 75 percent
(D) 100 percent

461. Which paragraph would benefit most from supporting evidence in the graphic?

(A) Paragraph 2
(B) Paragraph 3
(C) Paragraph 5
(D) Paragraph 6

Passage 18

Leonardo DaVinci might be best known for his paintings the *Mona Lisa* and *The Last Supper*, but he actually spent most of his time thinking up and inventing new machines. Sometimes considered the original "Renaissance Man" by scholars, DaVinci was an artist, a scientist, an architect, a teacher, an engineer, and an inventor. He was also centuries ahead of his time in his studies of human anatomy. Few people knew this because <u>DaVinci was born out of wedlock,</u> and
462
his social status prevented him from getting higher formal education, well-paying jobs, or access to connections that <u>might have gotten</u> him published.
463
When DaVinci was 15, he was apprenticed to a painter in Florence, Italy. During this time, he learned and refined his artistic skills that would benefit his future work and make him a singularly unique man. In 1482, he moved to the city of Milan, primarily a "war city," and <u>convinces</u> the Duke of Milan to hire
464
him as a military engineer. For the next 17 years, DaVinci designed and built

war machines and aqueducts, and spent the rest of his time painting, sculpting, inventing, studying science, and conceiving new ideas for machines. <u>Way ahead of his time in understanding the applications of force, gravity, and the biomechanics of the human body, many of his inventions could be considered precursors to modern technology.</u>
465

One invention DaVinci improved upon was the anemometer. This device measured wind speed, and he improved it to make it more accurate for measuring not only the speed but the force as well. Today, anemometers are essential in the study of meteorology. He also designed the "Aerial Screw" that had a spiral frame that was covered <u>in silk and</u> when turned with a crank, the
466
spiral would revolve, creating lift. This was a concept later used in helicopters. He invented a flying machine <u>that's</u> wings were framed in lightweight wood and
467
covered with linen or silk. A pilot would lie on a platform between the wings and turn a crank that made them move up and down. DaVinci based the design for these wings on a bat's wings. They also incorporated a twisting motion, not just the vertical motion that would later be applied to steering and changing altitudes. There is no evidence the machine was ever built, but no human would ever be able to crank it fast enough to get off the ground.

[1] DaVinci's concepts and inventions number into the hundreds, <u>but</u>
468
when people built these inventions based on his original designs, most of them worked. [2] But it was his studies into the human body that could have revolutionized science. [3] DaVinci performed close to 30 autopsies in his lifetime. [4] These autopsies led to comprehensive works on the anatomy of the human body and the understanding of how the body systems functioned together as moving parts. [5] He began with sketches of the human skull, and over the years compiled a collection of 240 drawings with over 13,000 words of notes into a manuscript called *Anatomical Manuscript A.*

He was most interested in understanding the structure of the heart. DaVinci was the first person to state it had four chambers and that the atria and ventricles moved with opposing forces, alternately contracting and relaxing to pump the blood. Had DaVinci been able to publish his works, modern medicine might have evolved centuries earlier. His set of skills as an artist combined with his discoveries make him a unique figure in <u>history, and</u> to this day, medical
₄₇₀
students often refer to his sketches as being more intricate than those in many standardized text books.

462. The author is considering deleting the underlined words. Which option provides the best support for this decision?

(A) No, because it explains his social status
(B) Yes, because it is private information
(C) No, because it is the only information about his parents
(D) Yes, because the detail is irrelevant

463.

(A) No change
(B) might get
(C) got
(D) could get

464.

(A) No change
(B) convinced
(C) convincing
(D) convince

465. Which option best revises the underlined sentence for clarity and conciseness?

(A) No change
(B) Many of his inventions could be considered precursors to modern technology because he was way ahead of his time in understanding the applications of force, gravity, and the biomechanics of the human body.
(C) Many of his inventions were way ahead of his time, understanding the applications of force, gravity, and the biomechanics of the human body, and precursors to modern technology.
(D) His understanding of the applications of force, gravity, and the biomechanics of the human body led to inventions that were precursors to modern technology.

466.

    (A) No change
    (B) silk, and
    (C) silk and,
    (D) silk, and,

467.

    (A) No change
    (B) that's
    (C) whose
    (D) who's

468.

    (A) No change
    (B) so
    (C) therefore
    (D) and

469. The author wants to include the following sentence in paragraph 4: "He had the first accurate depiction of the spinal cord and the earliest known description of cirrhosis of the liver." Which location is the most logical choice?

    (A) After sentence 2
    (B) After sentence 3
    (C) After sentence 4
    (D) After sentence 5

470.

    (A) No change
    (B) history and,
    (C) history, and,
    (D) history and

Passage 19

After graduating college, I realized I wanted to have my own place, be able to travel, live a <u>more eco-friendly</u> lifestyle, escape from the world once in a while,
                    471
and still be able to pay for it all without going into more debt. The more research I did, the more I realized I had two options: off-grid or tiny house living. Both options were way more involved than just selling all my stuff, hopping into my

truck, and taking off down the open road. I had to consider location, budget, resources, energy production, food, water, land, zoning laws, and why I wanted to live this lifestyle in the first place.

People decide to live off the grid or in tiny houses for a variety of reasons. For some people, <u>its</u> a financial situation. They don't want a mortgage or the
472
high cost of utilities and maintenance associated with a larger home. A person might have lost his or her job, and with little to no income, this might be the only option. Some people want to live more sustainable lives and reduce their carbon footprints, and others want to completely escape society and become "untraceable." Living off the grid means different things depending on which "grid" you are trying to get away from. Some tiny houses are <u>"off-grid," and</u>
473
others are merely tiny versions of a regular home with scaled down amenities.

I had to think about my goals. I wanted low maintenance, energy efficiency, optional permanence, and a sense of security. A tent or RV might suit some people, but it would not meet my needs. A tiny house would have options to fit exactly what I wanted. With homes as small as 100 square feet, I would definitely be able to declutter my life and maintain the space. Tiny houses use significantly less energy, and with optional solar panels or wind turbines for alternative energy, it would be much less expensive than a single-family home or apartment. Water <u>should</u> be an issue, but a tiny home could be connected
474
to a well, and some roofs could be designed to harvest rainwater and store it in barrels. A plot of land to park it on and a trailer to tow it <u>offers</u> options for
475
multiple locations.

Some tiny houses can be purchased or built for less than $15,000, depending on materials, so it could be purchased outright instead of getting a loan. Do-it-yourself kits can save thousands, but without construction experience, they are not recommended. Depending on materials, finishings, and labor, a person could

spend more than $100,000 on a tiny house! Sometimes it is less expensive to convert an existing structure like a shipping container, a horse trailer, or a shed. But off-grid living, whether in a tiny house or <u>living primitively</u>, is not legal
<u>477</u>
everywhere and not always economically viable. <u>States and cities have different</u>
<u>zoning laws, varying tax rates for residential and agricultural properties, different</u>
478
<u>requirements for being hooked up to city utilities like electrical or sewer systems,</u>
<u>and land prices can be drastically different depending on how close they are to</u>
<u>major cities.</u>

[479] Using these guidelines, <u>I narrowed down, for tiny houses, the top</u>
<u>states to live in to five.</u> Northern California has mild climates, plenty of water sources, lower taxes, and less strict land ordinances. Prices are fair, but not cheap. Northern Arizona has cheap land and great weather, but access to water could be an issue. New Hampshire, if you can deal with long, cold, snowy winters,
<u>are cheap</u>. It has the most affordable land (much of it remote with tons of natural
480
resources for food, heat, and water), legal off-grid zoning and reasonable building codes, and the lowest state and property taxes in the country. Finally, Florida, despite rumors, has made off-grid and tiny house living the most accessible, especially in rural areas. Proper septic tanks and clean water are required, but land is affordable, and residents can have solar panels and wind turbines for energy, water wells, gardens, and even livestock to remain self-sufficient. Wherever I end up calling home, off-grid and tiny house living offer better health, more financial freedom, less stress, and greater personal satisfaction than mainstream living.

471.

    (A) No change
    (B) eco-friendlier
    (C) eco friendly
    (D) more eco-friendlier

472.

    (A) No change

    (B) it's

    (C) thats

    (D) that's

473.

    (A) No change

    (B) "off-grid"—and

    (C) "off-grid," and

    (D) "off-grid"; and

474.

    (A) No change

    (B) could

    (C) would

    (D) won't

475.

    (A) No change

    (B) offered

    (C) are offering

    (D) offer

476. Which paragraph would be the best location for the following sentence? "An off-grid homestead could be established on as little as a half-acre of land, ideally with some woodland, good exposure to sunlight for solar power, a water source, and enough land for farming or a garden."

    (A) Paragraph 2

    (B) Paragraph 3

    (C) Paragraph 4

    (D) Paragraph 5

477.

    (A) No change

    (B) more primitively

    (C) more primitive living

    (D) living more primitively

478. Where could the underlined sentence be divided to improve flow and clarity?

(A) Between *systems* and *land*

(B) Between *laws* and *varying*

(C) between *land* and *prices*

(D) between *properties* and *different*

479. Which option best revises the underlined sentence for clarity?

(A) No change

(B) Using these guidelines, I narrowed down the top five best states to live in for tiny houses and off-grid lifestyles.

(C) Using these guidelines, the top best states to live in for tiny houses and off-grid lifestyles was narrowed to five.

(D) I narrowed down the best states to live in to five, using these guidelines for tiny house and off-grid living.

480.

(A) No change

(B) is cheapest

(C) are cheapest

(D) are cheaper

Passage 20

On the island of Kauai, in Hawaii, the running joke is that their "official" bird

<u>are</u> the chicken. Here, chickens are truly free range, living wherever they
481

<u>want, and</u> eating everything from garbage to cat food. Some are fed by tourists
482

and others forage in nature. Some locals <u>blames</u> Hurricane Iwa in 1982 and
483

others, a subsequent hurricane (10 years later) for blowing open the coops

of domestic birds and allowing them to escape and breed with the wild Red

Junglefowl. The Audubon Society reports an increase in the number of birds

after every hurricane. <u>However it happened,</u> chickens are running amok on the
484

island and causing all kinds of problems.

The word *dangerous* is not the first one that comes to mind when thinking

about chickens, but the rampant <u>presents</u> of the bird gives the residents of Kauai
485

more than a little grief when the crowing starts at 2:00 a.m. and goes on for hours. The birds destroy gardens and landscaping, scratching at roots and small plants; eating fruits, vegetables, and seeds; and costing people money in lost produce or revenue and repair costs. They poop anywhere and everywhere, and bird poop contains bacteria that can cause many illnesses; it can even kill native bird species. These chickens are often more aggressive than native birds and can kill them. They also cause traffic jams and accidents when flocking in the middle of the roads. But the chickens do eat a lot of bugs, including the Hawaiian stinging centipede. Tourists love them, and chicken souvenirs bring in a lot of money to the local economy.

[1] Chickens are not native to Kauai in the sense that they have always been on the island. [2] The Red Junglefowl is a semi-domesticated cousin of Southeast Asian pheasants that <u>were</u> brought to the islands of Hawaii when the Polynesians
486
arrived. [3] DNA tests of random chickens found around the island match some of the DNA from these fossils. [4] Anthropologists are using the chicken DNA to help track Polynesian expansion across the globe, because history shows they never traveled without their chickens.

Ornithologists are studying Kauai's birds because these chickens have evolved on the island for hundreds of years, with no outside DNA tainting the birds. <u>Feralization traditionally occurs just the opposite of domestication</u>. However,
488
interbreeding between the Red Junglefowl and the domestic chicken <u>are</u> having
489
some interesting results. Chickens are taking on some of the more ancient traits, like smaller size, colorful appearances, and the instinct to brood on a nest, but keeping some of the more domestic traits, including smaller brain sizes.

One reason Kauai is having difficulty controlling its chicken population is a lack of natural predators on the island. When European and American settlers came to the islands, they brought the mongoose, which ultimately wiped out almost the entire chicken population of Hawaii except on Kauai and Niihau.

Still, on the island of Oahu, people trap and kill dozens of feral chickens every

year. The Humane Society used to provide traps, but the demand was so high,

it referred people to the internet for the traps. For a $5 donation, it will pick up

the birds. Birds that are healthy are offered to people to eat as a sustainable food

source. The issue has been discussed many times at local and state government

levels, but it still causes much conflict. In Kauai, the chicken is ultimately

representative of a history and culture that defines the island and its inhabitants,

and no one is anxious to see <u>them</u> disappear.
490

481.

    (A) No change
    (B) was
    (C) is
    (D) were

482.

    (A) No change
    (B) want and,
    (C) want and
    (D) want; and

483.

    (A) No change
    (B) blamed
    (C) blaming
    (D) blame

484.

    (A) No change
    (B) However, it happened
    (C) How ever it happened,
    (D) How ever, it happened

485.

    (A) No change
    (B) presence
    (C) presense
    (D) precense

486.

(A) No change
(B) had
(C) was
(D) been

487. Which option is the most logical placement in paragraph 3 for the following sentence "Chicken fossils found on the island date back about 800 years."

(A) After sentence 1
(B) After sentence 2
(C) After sentence 3
(D) After sentence 4

488. The author is considering deleting the underlined sentence. Is this a good option?

(A) Yes, because it does not specifically reference what is happening with the chickens
(B) Yes, because it offers no definitions for the words
(C) No, because it explains the process of how the chickens are going wild
(D) No, because it explains why scientists are surprised by the chicken DNA

489.

(A) No change
(B) were
(C) is
(D) was

490.

(A) No change
(B) it
(C) us
(D) any

Passage 21

The yogurt industry is growing almost faster than any other grocery staple in the United States. In 2010, yogurt was a $4.5 billion industry that <u>grows</u> to
221
$8.5 billion in 2017. So how did this happen? Creative marketing campaigns by big companies offer one explanation. Dannon, which currently has 34

percent of the US yogurt market, originally made yogurt a mainstream food in the American diet back in the 1970s. It first distributed yogurt in 1942, but <u>popularity did not increase until the addition of a layer of fruit on the bottom in 1947.</u> Dannon expanded distribution nationally in the 1960s, but it was a
492
commercial in the 1970s that began the yogurt revolution. Barat Tabahra, an 89-year-old Soviet immigrant, went on television and <u>telling</u> the world his long
493
life, and that of his mother, age 114, was due to eating yogurt every day.

For 75 years, Dannon has continued to expand, and holds the majority of the yogurt industry in the United States. The main reason for this is <u>diversification.</u>
494
<u>Dannon has</u> more brand names and types of yogurt than any other company. Its corporation includes Dannon, Activia, Stonyfield Farms, Danimals, YoCrunch, and Oikos, as well as new yogurt drinks and smoothies. Dannon offers yogurts <u>produced</u> to appeal to the various demographics across the country, including
495
children, athletes, and on-the-go professionals. And Dannon isn't the only company leaving a large footprint in the yogurt business.

Yogurt has a long history, at least in Europe and the Mediterranean, of being a healthy staple in their cuisines. So it comes as no surprise that yogurt companies are creating yogurt brands, styles, and ad campaigns to appeal to the different needs of consumers. The potential health benefits of yogurt include promoting healthy digestion, lowering the risk of type 2 diabetes, protection against colorectal cancer, protection and treatment of osteoporosis, increased weight loss, and reduced high blood pressure and bad cholesterol. Yogurt alone can't cure all <u>ills, but</u> as "part of a healthy diet combined with exercise," it offers a much
496
healthier snack with numerous options that <u>had never been</u> available.
497
Ten years ago, no one had heard of Greek yogurt. It represented less than 1 percent of nationwide yogurt sales. Chobani, now a household name in Greek yogurt, began to emerge into the market in 2007. So what strategy was used to bring Greek yogurt from 1 percent of the market to almost half? Chief marketing

officer for Chobani, Peter McGuiness, decided the company needed a new approach, and began to hold yogurt tastings. Food sales increase exponentially when people get to interact with the food, do taste comparisons, and build
<u>498</u>
relationships with the company. Greek yogurt represented $1.5 billion of the total yogurt sales for 2017.

Yogurt is still a growing business. It is less expensive than most other snacks and has many alleged health benefits. <u>Convenience drives the market.</u>
<u>500</u>
<u>Available in cups, bottles, pouches, tubs, and tubes.</u> In the last five years, joining the variety of flavors, low fat, nonfat, blended, and Greek <u>will be</u> Icelandic, Australian, coconut milk, soy milk, strained, and organic. With a yogurt for every taste, the yogurt industry can rest assured that profits will continue to grow along with consumer appetites.

491.
    (A) No change
    (B) growed
    (C) grew
    (D) growing

492. Which option best revises the underline phrase for conciseness?
    (A) No change
    (B) popularity did not increase until 1947 with the addition of a layer of fruit on the bottom.
    (C) the addition of a layer of fruit on the bottom increased popularity in 1947.
    (D) in 1947, popularity increased when a layer of fruit was added on the bottom.

493.
    (A) No change
    (B) told
    (C) tells
    (D) tell

494. Which option best combines the two sentences?
    (A) diversification, and
    (B) diversification but
    (C) diversification; and
    (D) diversification, so

495.

    (A) No change

    (B) tested

    (C) made

    (D) marketed

496.

    (A) No change

    (B) ills but

    (C) ills but,

    (D) ills, but,

497.

    (A) No change

    (B) were never

    (C) were not

    (D) was not

498.

    (A) No change

    (B) delete completely

    (C) got to

    (D) have to

499. Which paragraph is the best fit for the following sentence? "Not just for breakfast anymore, yogurt is replacing snacks, meals, and even desserts."

    (A) Paragraph 2

    (B) Paragraph 3

    (C) Paragraph 4

    (D) Paragraph 5

500. Which option best combines the underlined sentences?

    (A) Convenience drives the market, and now it's available in cups, bottles, pouches, tubs, and tubes.

    (B) Available in cups, bottles, pouches, tubs, and tubes, convenience drives the market.

    (C) The market is driven by convenience so there are cups, bottles, pouches, tubs, and tubes for yogurt.

    (D) Cups, bottles, pouches, tubs, and tubes make yogurt convenient, which drives the market.

ANSWERS

Critical Reading Answers

Passage 1

1. **(C)** The statement "Many companies refuse to hire workers younger than eighteen" is not supported in the text.

2. **(C)** The word *ineptitude* in line 19 most nearly means "incompetence."

3. **(A)** According to the passage, benevolent prejudice appears friendly and harmless.

4. **(C)** The statement "There is more than one kind of age-related bias" is true about ageism.

5. **(B)** The word *manifests* in line 18 most nearly means "reveals."

6. **(D)** The statement that is not true is "there are some jobs that could be too physically demanding for an elderly employee."

7. **(B)** The word *insidious* in line 20 most nearly means "sinister."

8. **(A)** The author's attitude toward ageism can best be described as appalled because *appalled* means "sickened or disgusted."

9. **(B)** The second paragraph mostly serves to give examples of benevolent prejudice, behaviors that seem harmless but are really prejudiced.

10. **(C)** The statement that is not true is "to convince employers to hire elderly workers," because the author is addressing forms of prejudice, not employers.

Passage 2

11. **(B)** The statement with which the author would most likely agree is that honeybees are affected by a number of ailments other than CCD.

12. **(B)** That "the pollination of luxury crops keeps bees from pollinating wild plants" is not a cause of CCD.

13. **(B)** The word *attrition* in line 14 most nearly means "reduction."

14. **(C)** It can be inferred from the first paragraph that the causes of CCD are complex, which is why research has shown that one single trigger is not a likely scenario.

15. (B) The "symbiotic relationship" of bees and plants (line 28) is analogous to cleaner shrimp that feed off the bacteria living on bigger fish that would otherwise make the bigger fish sick; *symbiotic* means "working together."

16. (B) In the last paragraph, the word *staples* most likely refers to common foods we eat.

17. (B) The statement that is not considered "acceptable winter loss" conditions is "the hive was destroyed by snowplows," because this scenario is unlikely to occur.

18. (C) The *overall* trend seen in bee colony losses from 2006–2016 is a general increase in all loss amounts.

19. (D) Prior to 2010–2011, it can be inferred that scientists realized there were other causes for the loss of bees, in addition to winter.

20. (C) Looking at the graph, the author of the passage would most likely agree that "little change in winter loss" means some other factor is killing the bees.

Passage 3

21. (B) The purpose of the first paragraph is to describe, in detail, the type of world that Belle Morgan stepped in to.

22. (B) As used in line 4, the word *supercilious* most nearly means "pompous."

23. (A) In line 7, the expression "our first families" is analogous to the British colonists of the Americas who first settled in the area.

24. (D) As used in line 8, the word *decorous* most nearly means "well-behaved."

25. (A) The narrator uses the clause "ennui claimed him for its own" to mean that Lennox was immensely bored by the end of the first week; *ennui* means "lethargy or boredom."

26. (D) It can be inferred from the passage that Belle was the girl in the scarlet stockings.

27. (B) As used in line 10, the word *irradicable* most nearly means "entrenched."

28. (D) According to the passage, Belle cannot be described as meager because *meager* means "scarce or small."

29. (C) According to lines 28–30, the statement "She enchanted and delighted everyone she passed" best describes Belle's effect on people in the street.

30. (B) As used in line 39, the word *elastic* most nearly means "flexible."

31. (D) In lines 33–36, the author suggests that Belle's presence is a complete contrast to her surroundings because she is described as "waking up the street and leaving a wake of sunshine."

32. (D) The statements that best describe the reason why the narrator calls Belle "a busy, bustling little body" in line 25 are as follows: "I. She was walking briskly to an unknown destination," and "III. Her hands and pockets were full of packages."

33. (C) The narrator suggests Lennox watches Belle pass by his window every day at three PM.

34. (B) "Lennox was usually the heartbreaker, but this time, a girl had caught his heart."

35. (D) The word *affectations* most nearly means "mannerisms."

Passage 4A & B

36. (B) The word *deficit* most nearly means "scarcity."

37. (B) The author describes the records of the 1890 census as *inimitable* because they contained unique information that would have given us new insights into American life.

38. (D) The census was *not* printed in several languages, only English.

39. (D) The word *vigilant* most nearly means "attentive."

40. (A) As a result of the fire, a special building was built to properly store archives.

41. (C) The author's purpose in Passage 4B is to give a brief history of the National Archives Building and its purpose.

42. (B) The word *spurred* most nearly means "incited."

43. (C) Neither author would agree to destroy original documents.

44. (C) People might use the National Archives Building to research their family's immigration history and obtain military benefits.

45. (C) It can be inferred that the author believes seeing the Declaration of Independence and the Constitution of the United States is best done in person.

Passage 5A & B

46. (C) The statement "The Navajo language was successful because few people in the world could understand it" can be inferred from Passage 5A because it says the language was unwritten and only spoken on Navajo lands.

47. (A) The main point of Passage 5B is that although the Navajo soldiers are the most renowned, they were not the original code talkers.

48. (D) The author of Passage 5A mentions the admission by the Japanese chief of intelligence in order to emphasize just how successful the use of Navajo was as a code.

49. (C) As used in paragraph 2 of Passage 5B, the word *hunch* most nearly means "intuition."

50. (B) The statement that most accurately describes the relationship between Passage 5A and Passage 5B is that both passages arrive at the same conclusion through different analyses.

51. (C) As used in paragraph 3 of Passage 5A, the word *exploits* most nearly means "courageous acts."

52. (B) The purpose of paragraph 1 in Passage 5B is to explain the renown of Navajo code talkers in society today.

53. (B) The author of Passage 5B would most likely respond to the conclusion of Passage 1 by pointing out that Choctaw soldiers still do not receive the same recognition as Navajo soldiers.

54. (B) As used in paragraph 3 of Passage 5A, the word *fanfare* most nearly means "celebration."

55. (A) The author of Passage 5B implies in paragraph 2 that although Choctaw was used openly, it was never deciphered by the Germans.

56. (A) It can be inferred from the passages that both authors would agree that the US Army owes many victories to the Native American code talkers.

57. (D) The author of Passage 5A would most likely agree that Navajo was the most successful military code in modern history.

58. (C) As used in paragraph 2 of Passage 5B, the word *company* refers to a military unit.

Passage 6

59. (C) It can be inferred from the passage that death rates for all smoking-related cancers are on the rise for women.

60. (D) As used in line 1, the word *diminishing* most nearly means "shrinking."

61. (B) The passage supports the idea that regional differences in lung cancer trends highlight the success of tobacco control programs.

62. (A) The second paragraph mostly serves to explain why different states and regions have different lung cancer death rates.

63. (B) As used in paragraph 2, the word *pervasiveness* most nearly means "ubiquity."

64. (C) The primary purpose of the passage is to provide an update on cancer trends, specifically smoking-related lung cancer.

65. (B) "We must accelerate and improve our efforts in reducing the burden of cancer in this country" is not supported by an explicit statement in the passage.

66. (A) The conclusion implies that efforts in prevention, early detection, and treatment should be frequently evaluated and improved.

67. (A) Another example of the "environmental factors" mentioned in paragraph 3 is pollution from automobiles.

68. (D) As used in the last sentence, the word *augment* most nearly means "to expand."

69. (A) The table supports that California and Utah populations have the lowest percentage of smokers.

70. (A) The author most likely did *not* use the statement "West Virginia's smoking population percentage and estimated cancer-related deaths are the highest" to support his argument.

Passage 7

71. (A) The statement "To reduce energy costs, air-conditioning systems should be turned on only when the room's temperature rises above 70 degrees" cannot be inferred from the passage.

72. (C) An "involuntary function" performed by the human body includes breathing.

73. (C) The author mentions reptiles in lines 4–5 in order to provide a comparison in the way that different species deal with temperature changes.

74. (C) In paragraph 2, the word *homeostasis* most likely means "maintaining a constant condition."

75. (B) The "core" described in paragraph 3 is most analogous to the body's center.

76. (D) The purpose of paragraphs 2 and 3 is to illustrate the body's natural protections from temperature.

77. (A) As used in paragraph 4, the word *ambient* most nearly means "surrounding."

78. (D) A person exhibiting the symptoms of an upset stomach, headache, and dizziness might be suffering from mild overheating.

79. (A) In paragraph 3, the word *disperse* most nearly means "diffuse."

80. (D) The author's purpose for this passage is most likely to explain the body's natural cooling system and the dangers of overheating.

Passage 8A & B

81. (D) The author's primary purpose in writing Passage 8A is to describe the history of female soldiers in the Civil War.

82. (A) As used in line 8 of Passage 8A, the word *unconventional* most nearly means "unusual."

83. (B) The author of Passage 8B would agree with the statement "The existence of soldier-women was no secret during or after the Civil War."

84. (A) The author of Passage 8B mentions Mary Owens in order to provide evidence of eyewitness accounts and published reports.

85. (C) As used in line 12 of Passage 8B, the word *fascination* most nearly means "interest."

86. (A) The authors of both passages discuss women who fought in the Union and Confederate armies.

87. (D) In lines 15–16, the author of Passage 8A suggests reasons why women were able to successfully pass as men in army camps by changing their names and wearing men's uniforms.

88. (A) The attitude of the author of Passage 8A toward women who fought in the Civil War can best be described as reverent because *reverent* means "respectful."

89. (A) In lines 12–15 of Passage 8B, the author implies that Mary Owens could have remained in service had she not been wounded.

90. (D) As used in line 8 of Passage 8A, the word *embedded* most nearly means "rooted."

91. (C) Both passages address different aspects of the same topic.

92. (A) "Rank and file" best describes the ordinary soldiers of the army, excluding officers.

93. (B) As used in line 36 of Passage 8B, the word *unscathed* most nearly means "unharmed."

Passage 9

94. (B) In lines 1–2, the narrator uses the phrase "ripe but well-cared-for" to describe the ladies at lunch.

95. (D) As used in line 3, the word *parapet* most nearly means "wall."

96. (B) The narrator's description of the people in lines 7–8 suggests that they are tourists.

97. (A) It can be inferred from the passage that the scene takes place in the late afternoon, because the waiter asked if the ladies would remain until dinner.

98. (B) As used in line 7, the word *extremity* most nearly means "edge."

99. (A) Mrs. Slade has "a retrospective smile" because she is recalling the past.

100. (A) In line 28, the narrator uses the phrase "as opulent-looking as Mrs. Ansley's" to suggest that both ladies are well-to-do women in society.

101. (B) In paragraph 7, lines 27–33, the narrator implies that Mrs. Slade addresses the headwaiter condescendingly.

102. (D) In the comparison in lines 25–26, the narrator suggests that Mrs. Slade is more gregarious and confident than Mrs. Ansley, because Mrs. Ansley blushes.

103. (A) In line 26, the narrator suggests that Mrs. Ansley never meant for her comment to be heard by Mrs. Slade.

104. (C) In the last sentence, Mrs. Ansley reveals that she is surprised because she did not think Mrs. Slade would be emotional about their youthful adventures.

105. (D) In the passage, the moonlight is used by the author as a symbol of youth and romance.

106. (A) As used in line 47, the word *sentimental* most nearly means "maudlin."

Passage 10

107. (B) The statement that best supports the main point of the passage is "Reducing incarceration rates will reduce poverty levels and improve the economy."

108. (B) As used in line 5, the word *efficacy* most nearly means "competence."

109. (B) Based on the second paragraph, the author would most likely agree with the statement "The United States has more nonviolent criminals in jail than violent criminals."

110. (A) The first paragraph serves mostly to exculpate the failures of the US judicial system by detailing how they haven't worked.

111. (C) In paragraph 2, the word *disproportionately* most nearly means "unreasonably."

112. (A) In the third paragraph, the author suggests that the increase of incarceration in America is felt most strongly by minorities.

113. (D) In paragraph 3, the word *direst* most nearly means "severest."

114. (C) The author mentions the aging prison population in order to provide another reason for the current US jail population crisis.

115. (C) In paragraph 4, it could be inferred that the author believes the money spent on lifelong prisoners might be better used elsewhere.

116. (A) Based on the table, the statement "States with higher incarceration rates have higher poverty levels" is true.

117. (C) It could be inferred from the table that poverty levels are strong indicators of higher crime rates and prison populations.

Passage 11

118. (B) The main purpose of the passage is to compare different theories about the origins of the moon.

119. (D) Paragraph 1 implies the moon has always played an important role in civilizations in many ways.

120. (D) In paragraph 3, the word *improbable* most nearly means "questionable."

121. (B) The statement "Condensation has to do with moisture, and there is no water in space" was not a discarded theory about the moon's origins.

122. (B) In paragraph 4, the word *coalesced* most nearly means "combined."

123. (C) The author would most like agree with the following statement: "Theories about the moon's origin will probably change as science improves its research abilities."

124. (D) In paragraph 4, the word *synchronous* most nearly means "simultaneous."

125. (C) In paragraphs 4–6, the author implies the collision between Earth and the other object was colossal.

126. (D) The purpose of the text in paragraph 6 is to provide evidence that directly relates to the newest theories of the moon's creation.

127. (B) It can be inferred from the passage that the author believes there are several possible causes for there being just one moon orbiting Earth.

Passage 12

128. (D) The author's primary purpose is to argue for the reduction of pollution through a decrease in beef production.

129. (B) The conclusion above is flawed because it doesn't take into account other methods of reducing greenhouse gas emissions.

130. (A) As used in paragraph 1, the word *copious* most nearly means "profuse."

131. (B) It can be inferred that "beef production generates a lot of greenhouse gases because the cattle release large amounts of methane."

132. (A) The author would most likely agree with the statement "Beef production generates more greenhouse gases than production of any other food we consume."

133. (B) As used in paragraph 2, the word *detrimentally* most nearly means "destructively."

134. (C) The purpose of paragraph 4 is to provide evidence of how cattle farming impacts the land.

135. (B) As used paragraph 1, the word *ominous* most nearly means "dire."

136. (B) The primary purpose of the fifth paragraph is to explain the growing scale of the beef production industry.

137. (C) As used in paragraph 4, the word *subsequently* most nearly means "afterward."

138. (C) In paragraph 2, the main idea is that farming results in contaminated water that can affect entire ecosystems.

139. (B) According to the passage, methane is a serious environmental concern because its potential effect on the environment is many times greater than that of carbon dioxide.

140. (C) As used in paragraph 5, the word *spurring* most nearly means "motivating."

Passage 13A & B

141. (A) The authors of both passages describe the acquisition of antiquities.

142. (B) As used in paragraph 1 of Passage 13A, the word *bequeathed* most nearly means "donated."

143. (D) It can be inferred from lines 16–17 of Passage 13A that the British Museum's collection today contains 50,000 objects.

144. (A) "The British Museum actively supported excavations in the twentieth century" best describes the changes mentioned in lines 14–15 of Passage 13A.

145. (C) The author's primary purpose in writing Passage 13B is to criticize the continued ownership of stolen antiquities.

146. (C) According to Passage 13A, the statement "The museum has more than 12 million objects in its Egyptian collections" is *not* true about the British Museum.

147. (D) The statement "The UNESCO convention is a robust international agreement regarding antiquities" is *not* supported by the third paragraph of Passage 13B.

148. (D) "The passages discuss the same topics, but they focus on different aspects of the topics" most accurately describes the relationship between Passages 13A and 13B.

149. (D) As used in paragraph 4 in Passage 13A, the word *repatriate* most nearly means "export."

150. (C) It can be inferred from Passage 13A that "The Rosetta Stone was the most important Egyptian artifact ever recovered."

151. (C) As used in paragraph 1 of Passage 13B, the word *unabated* most nearly means "unhindered."

152. (C) As used in line 26 of Passage 13B, the word *pilfered* most nearly means "stolen."

153. (C) Paragraph 2 of Passage 13B implies the loss of national cultural and historical treasures affects countries in multiple ways.

Passage 14

154. (A) The passage is written in the first-person point of view.

155. (D) The treatments for the speaker's condition involve all of the following *except* isolation.

156. (C) The repetition of the word *personally* implies she is amused by her husband's and brother's opinions.

157. (B) The word *draught* most nearly means "a draft."

158. (C) The narrator's tone when describing the house can be best characterized as romantic and whimsical.

159. (A) The speaker most desires to spend her time writing.

160. **(A)** The word *flamboyant* most nearly means "gaudy."

161. **(A)** The speaker's husband is best described as controlling and pragmatic.

162. **(B)** The narrator's attitude toward her husband's treatment of her might best be described as resigned.

163. **(D)** The speaker's "slight hysterical tendencies" are most clearly demonstrated by her obsession with the wallpaper in her room.

164. **(D)** One major similarity between the narrator's room and the wallpaper's pattern is that they both have bars.

165. **(B)** "The Yellow Wallpaper" is written in the style of a stream of consciousness.

Passage 15

166. **(B)** As used in paragraph 2, the word *dwindling* most nearly means "decreasing."

167. **(D)** The statements that best support the main passage are "Fresh water is being used up faster than it is being replaced," and "There are many methods of reducing excess water use."

168. **(C)** The main purpose of paragraph 2 is to explain what an aquifer is and how it is impacted by shrinking water resources.

169. **(B)** The harmful effects of desalination to the environment are *not* mentioned as a possible cause of decreased availability of freshwater.

170. **(B)** As used in paragraph 2, the word *porous* most nearly means "absorbent."

171. **(A)** Paragraph 4 suggests that the author believes that desalination is a problematic and unwise solution because the passage states that it is a costly process and the plants create more pollution.

172. **(A)** In paragraph 2 the word *consumption* most nearly means "ingestion."

173. **(C)** All of the following are strategies to improve water efficiency *except* leaving the water on cold when you wash dishes or brush your teeth.

174. **(B)** The author would most likely agree with the statement "the water crisis needs to be addressed on a global scale."

175. **(C)** The main purpose of this passage is to look at the dangers, causes, and potential solutions to the freshwater crisis.

176. **(C)** In paragraph 4, all of the following words are synonyms for *laudable except* "ineffectual."

177. **(D)** The tone of the passage is urgent.

Passage 16

178. (D) The main purpose of the passage is to honor all of the various areas of knowledge and skills that went into designing and building the bridge.

179. (A) Passage 1 implies that science was not advanced enough to build this bridge until now because it states directly, "In no previous period of the world's history could this bridge have been built."

180. (C) In paragraph 1, "intricate laws of force" refers to physics, because physics is the study of forces and their applications to the real world.

181. (A) In paragraph 1, the word *effectually* most likely means "effectively."

182. (C) The main purpose of paragraph 2 is to illustrate how much skill and information was required to build this bridge.

183. (D) In paragraph 2, the word *ingenuity* most nearly means "creativity."

184. (B) The overall tone of the passage is grandiose and flamboyant.

185. (B) In the following quote, "Ah! what a wondrous thing it is to note how many wheels of toil one word, one thought can set in motion," the phrase "wheels of toil" is an example of metaphor.

186. (C) The speaker would most likely agree with all of the following statements *except* "The Brooklyn Bridge was still not big enough to accommodate all the traffic that would use it in the future."

187. (D) In paragraph 5, it can be inferred that "the moral qualities of the human soul" are patience, courage, and endurance because they are internal qualities that cannot be quantified.

188. (C) In paragraph 5, the word *execution* most likely means "the implementation of the plan."

Passage 17

189. (B) Based on the passage, the author would most likely describe the current energy crisis as a dangerous and urgent threat to global peace and economic stability.

190. (C) As used in paragraph 3, the word *prohibitively* most likely means "exorbitantly."

191. (A) In the third paragraph, the author suggests that unconventional methods of extracting crude oil are financially improbable.

192. (D) The statement "Producers will raise prices, which means the poor will be unable to purchase sufficient amounts of even the most basic food products" best describes the "problem" mentioned in the sixth paragraph.

193. (D) As used in paragraph 3, the word *precipitously* most nearly means "sharply."

194. (B) The statement "To describe the problems surrounding the development of alternative sources of energy" most accurately describes the purpose of the fourth paragraph.

195. (A) As used in paragraph 5, the word *marginalized* most nearly means "relegated."

196. (D) The statement "Hydrofracking allows for the extraction of infinite deposits of crude oil" is *not* supported by the passage.

197. (D) As used in the final paragraph, the word *dissemination* most nearly means "distribution."

198. (A) Paragraph 3 suggests that the author regards unconventional methods of extracting crude oil as new technologies that are essential, but experimental and divisive.

199. (D) The statement "Higher prices at the gas pump would go much further in convincing people to drive less" would reconcile the discrepancy in the last paragraph.

200. (C) The reason why some nations do not use nuclear power is because the effect of a plant meltdown would be too devastating.

Passage 18

201. (C) The statement "The internet has positive and negative aspects that should be considered carefully when using it" best supports the main point.

202. (B) The main purpose of paragraph 1 is to explain the field of Web science.

203. (D) The phrase "sharing private videos and photos with strangers" does not show the benefits of using social media.

204. (B) In paragraph 3, the word *rampant* most likely means "ubiquitous."

205. (C) The author would most likely agree with the statement "Social media companies should monitor their sites more closely for cyberbullying and take a stand against it."

206. (C) In paragraph 3, the word *inciting* most nearly means "provoking."

207. (C) The statement "it is easy to tamper with computer evidence" is not a reason cybercrime is difficult to prevent.

208. (B) Someone who commits identity theft might open credit cards in the victim's name.

209. (A) In paragraph 4, the word *havoc* most likely means "chaos."

210. (A) According to the graph, the statement "Cyberbullying has increased 2000 percent in less than a decade" is most likely true.

211. (D) The graph implies that more instances of cyberbullying are being reported, and advancing technology is making bullying easier.

212. (C) We can infer from the conclusion that people can take actions to protect themselves from cybercrime.

Passage 19

213. (C) In paragraph 1, the narrator, Giovanni, is "impressed . . . disagreeably" by the gardener's fear of touching his own plants.

214. (D) In paragraph 1, the word *demeanor* most likely means "disposition."

215. (C) In lines 6–12 of paragraph 1, it can be inferred that the gardener is careful because he knows the plants are dangerous.

216. (C) The quote "pruning the too luxuriant growth" does not support evidence for the previous answer because it does not indicate danger.

217. (B) Giovanni's description of Beatrice's voice as "a voice as rich as a tropical sunset" is an example of a simile.

218. (B) Giovanni's first impression of Beatrice is that she is almost too beautiful to be real.

219. (D) In paragraph 6, the word *morbid* most nearly means "sinister."

220. (B) In paragraph 6, Giovanni makes a disturbing observation that Beatrice touches the flowers and plants without gloves, unlike her father.

221. (C) It might be inferred from this passage that Giovanni has a vivid imagination.

222. (B) The word *consigned* most likely means "quarantined."

223. (A) The word *fraught* most nearly means "burdened."

224. (B) The final sentence of the passage foreshadows that Beatrice will be a danger to Giovanni.

Passage 20

225. (D) The phrase "gathering clouds and raging storms" most likely refers to the difficult challenges America faces, listed in the paragraph.

226. (B) The word *prosperity* most likely means "success."

227. (D) "The time has come to reaffirm our enduring spirit; to choose our better history; to carry forward that precious gift, that noble idea passed on from generation to generation: the God-given promise that all are equal, all are free, and all deserve a chance to pursue their full measure of happiness" implies the American dream is the greatest dream someone can have.

228. (B) "So it has been; so it must be" is an example of parallelism.

229. (B) The main point of paragraph 3 is to present examples of the struggles America is facing.

230. (C) The use of the word *inevitable* in paragraph 3 most likely means "fated."

231. (A) The word *dogma* most nearly means "doctrine."

232. (C) President Obama's purpose for speaking about the struggles and failures of America in paragraph 3 is most likely to show he is paying attention to the condition of life in the country and to the people who are experiencing it.

233. (D) The quote "The time has come to reaffirm our enduring spirit; to choose our better history; to carry forward that precious gift, that noble idea passed on from generation to generation: the God-given promise that all are equal, all are free, and all deserve a chance to pursue their full measure of happiness" implies that the American people must choose to work together to save the American dream and the ideas of freedom and happiness.

234. (B) In paragraph 6, the word *reaffirming* most nearly means "validating."

235. (C) Paragraphs 7–9 serve to emphasize the idea that America's greatness was earned through hard work and sacrifice.

236. (C) The main purpose of President Obama's speech was most likely to promise that his presidency will make positive change for the American people.

Passage 21

237. (C) The author will most likely agree with the statement "Hoarding is a debilitating behavioral condition."

238. (A) The statement "Hoarding is a relatively new syndrome for the mental health community to address" most supports the author's conclusion.

239. (A) As used in paragraph 1, the word *quotidian* most nearly means "commonplace," because cooking and watching TV are common activities.

240. (C) The first paragraph mostly serves to introduce the problem of hoarding.

241. (D) As used in paragraph 3, the word *escalate* most nearly means "intensify."

242. (D) Credit card debt is not a health hazard that results from hoarding.

243. (C) The author would most likely disagree with the statement "To stop a hoarder, just throw away all the stuff."

244. (B) In paragraph 4, the word *irreparable* most nearly means "permanent."

245. (A) According to paragraph 4, the statement "as long as you can afford it, it's not hoarding" is not a possible consequence of hoarding.

246. (B) The main purpose of paragraph 5 is to explain potential reasons for hoarding behavior.

247. (A) In paragraph 4, the word *denial* most nearly means "rejection."

248. (C) It would make the most sense to add the statement "Openly discussing hoarding behaviors can provide insight for doctors and researchers" to the final paragraph.

Passage 22A & B

249. (A) As used in Passage 22B, the word *specter* most nearly means "presence."

250. (A) The author's primary purpose in writing Passage 22A is to discuss opinions about plus-size fashion.

251. (C) The authors of the two passages would most likely disagree on whether the industry is responsible for how it markets products and images to society.

252. (A) As used in paragraph 2 of Passage 22A, the word *bombards* most nearly means "overwhelms."

253. (D) The author's attitude toward plus-size marketing in Passage 22A can best be described as antagonistic because the author talks about it as being unrealistic and damaging.

254. (B) As used in paragraph 2 of Passage 22B, the word *pernicious* most nearly means "destructive."

255. (B) The author would most likely agree with statement "The fashion industry should emphasize a trim, athletic figure as the ideal body type."

256. (B) As used in paragraph 3 of Passage 22B, the word *proactive* most nearly means "energetic."

257. (D) Both passages mention the fact that the fashion industry has been accused of portraying women's bodies through the media in ways that are harmful and unreasonable.

258. (A) As used in paragraph 3 of Passage 22A, the word *misnomer* most nearly means "an unsuitable term."

259. (B) In paragraph 3 of Passage 22B, the author suggests that "models with a BMI lower than 18 should not be allowed to walk any runways in European and Asian shows."

260. (B) Including actual quotes from models with eating disorders would make the conclusion of Passage 22B stronger.

Passage 23

261. (D) The statement that best summarizes a major theme of the selection is "There is no purpose in holding on to petty grudges" because the feud is the reason why the two men ended up trapped.

262. (D) The quote "Lying here tonight, thinking, I've come to think we've been rather fools. There are better things in life than getting the better of a boundary dispute" best supports the answer to the previous question because it indicates a change in perspective.

263. (A) The statement that best describes the relationship between Ulrich and Georg is "because of their families' feud, they both consider each other enemies and trespassers," as stated in the beginning of the passage.

264. (B) The phrase "the code of a restraining civilization" most likely refers to laws and regulations.

265. (C) In paragraph 1, the word *pinioned* most likely means "immobilized."

266. (D) The statement that best describes the irony of Georg and Ulrich's predicament is "They wanted to kill each other and now they are trapped and seriously injured together," because irony occurs when something happens that is unexpected or contradictory.

267. (C) In paragraph 10, the word *interlopers* most likely means "intruders."

268. (C) The main conflict in the passage is man versus man.

269. (B) The example of man versus man conflict is the long-standing feud between Georg and Ulrich.

270. (B) In the final paragraph, the word *compact* most likely means "agreement."

Writing & Language—Answers

Passage 1

271. (B) The writer should use "Today, dogs work with the police, military, in hospitals and nursing homes, and as service dogs to people with a variety of disabilities" to revise sentence 1 to improve clarity.

272. (A) The author shouldn't make any changes to sentence 2 because the use of punctuation is correct for both the apostrophe and the comma.

273. (B) The best option is *mobility impairments* because it is a noun and remains consistent with the list.

274. (C) The writer should use "They can be trained to sniff for guns, explosives, drugs, and to find survivors of natural disasters or dead bodies covered in rubble and wreckage" to improve conciseness and clarity in listing the skills of the dogs.

275. (A) There is no change because a colon can be used to indicate a following list.

276. (B) The best option is *retrieve* because the dog would bring assistance back to its owner.

277. (D) The best option is *provide* to maintain consistent subject–verb agreement in the sentence.

278. (B) The best option is *their*, to indicate possession.

279. (C) To make this paragraph the most logical, sentence 2 should be deleted from the paragraph because it does not offer details relevant to other information presented.

280. (C) The best option is *for*.

281. (C) The choice that most effectively combines the two sentences at the underlined portion is "train them, and these dogs" because it is inclusive and specifies the dogs enable people, not the trainers.

282. (B) The sentence "The number of adults in the United States reporting disabilities increased by 3.4 million between 1999 and 2005 and continues to rise" would provide more supporting evidence for the final paragraph.

Passage 2

283. (D) Using the option "Transportation and communication have made the global community smaller than ever" would make the introductory sentences more concise because it focuses on the main point.

284. (D) The phrase "tracing that heritage can be difficult" maintains a consistent verb in the sentence.

285. (A) No change is needed because the subject and verb are both singular.

286. (D) This is the best option to maintain the flow of the paragraph and clearly present the information.

287. (D) This sentence should be deleted because the information is presented in the previous sentence.

288. (C) This is the best option because it indicates that DNA was discovered and researched long before it was available and understandable to the general public.

289. (B) This option appropriately does not use an apostrophe with the decade, and it uses a comma after an independent clause (complete sentence).

290. (A) No change needs to be made.

291. (C) This option for sentence 2 best clarifies the previous sentence because it explains why test results might be misleading, but not wrong.

292. (D) The best option is *occasionally* because the sentences states "not often."

293. (C) This would be the best option to strengthen the conclusion because it summarizes the most important points of the paragraph without making unsubstantiated comments.

294. (A) The graph does not indicate when the companies started DNA testing. The graph only begins comparing them in 2012.

295. (B) Paragraph 2 would be strengthened using information from the graph because it compares both companies.

Passage 3

296. (A) No change is needed.

297. (B) Option B best presents the information in a clear and concise manner.

298. (B) The sentence should not be replaced because it begins to discuss important information about why the city needed the park; however, not enough information is there to support it.

299. (D) In the sentence, *parks* should not be capitalized.

300. (C) This is the best option because it clarifies the features are part of the reason residents and tourists enjoy the activities.

301. (A) No change is needed.

302. (B) The best option is *their* to indicate possession.

303. (A) No change is needed to improve the effectiveness of the paragraph.

304. (C) The best option is *decayed* to maintain consistent verb tense in the sentence.

305. (B) The best option is *seeped* because it indicates a slow increase over time.

306. (C) The best option is C to maintain pronoun–antecedent agreement between *the City of New York* and *its*.

307. (C) The best option is C because you would not use a semicolon with a conjunction to join two complete sentences.

Passage 4

308. (B) Option B is the best choice because you would not use *most* and *costliest* together.

309. (B) This sentence would work best as the first sentence of paragraph 2 because it indicates the start of new information.

310. (C) Option C is the best option because "which are not the same as blizzards" is a nonrestrictive clause that needs to be separated by commas.

311. (C) This sentence does not relate to or support any other information in the paragraph and should be deleted.

312. (C) Option C provides the most concise option to present the information in the sentence.

313. (A) No change is needed.

314. (D) Option D provides the clearest introduction to paragraph 4 because it specifically states the paragraph will discuss the aftermath of the storms.

315. (C) This option correctly joins two complete sentences with a comma and a conjunction.

316. (C) This option best revises the sentence to maintain consistent verb tense.

317. (A) No change is necessary. *Its* refers to climate change's impact.

318. (C) Based on the graph, rainfall appears to be the costliest factor of a superstorm.

319. (D) No information in the graph confirms the statement.

Passage 5

320. (B) Option B best revises the sentence for clarity and correct punctuation.

321. (C) Option C, *threatened,* is correct because it maintains consistent verb tense.

322. (B) This option offers the best transition because it introduces Isabella Stewart Gardner to the passage.

323. (D) *Began* is the correct option using past tense.

324. (C) This option correctly uses a comma between two complete sentences.

325. (B) *Motivated* is the best option because it refers to Isabella's internal, emotional, feelings.

326. (A) Option A is the best option as the passage refers to Isabella's will, which specifically states these instructions.

327. (D) The correct option is *their* because it refers to a plural antecedent.

328. (B) This is the best option because the previous sentence mentions theories.

329. (A) No change is necessary.

Passage 6

330. (D) The correct word is *lose. Loose* means "not tight."

331. (D) This is the best option to clearly express the narrator's thoughts.

332. (B) This is the correct option because the event occurred in the past.

333. (C) This is the correct option because the verb should be past tense.

334. (A) No change is necessary.

335. (D) Option D best combines the underlined phrases into one complete sentence to present the information.

336. (D) This is the correct option because *an* should generally be used when the following word begins with a vowel. It also uses the correct tense of the verb.

337. (C) This is the correct option because a semicolon would be used to connect two complete sentences without a conjunction.

338. (B) *Achieving* is the best option because it specifically indicates the narrator is working toward something.

339. (C) This is the best option to add the list as part of the previous sentence.

340. (B) Option B is most accurately represented by the graph.

341. (A) Information from the graph would be most effective if used in the second paragraph when discussing eating and shopping trends.

Passage 7

342. (B) *Uneventful* is the best option because the previous sentence indicates the opposite situation.

343. (A) No change necessary.

344. (A) No change necessary.

345. (C) The correct option is C because the verb should remain past tense.

346. (C) The correct option is after sentence 4, which details the qualities that helped him win the election.

347. (C) The correct answer is *its*, referring back to the administration.

348. (D) The best vocabulary option is *tainted*, meaning "spoiled or contaminated," whereas *labeled* does not have negative connotations.

349. (B) The best vocabulary option is *revealed* because it was previously unknown.

350. (D) The best option to connect two complete sentences is D, using a semicolon.

351. (B) The best option is B, using *which* as part of a restrictive clause.

Passage 8

352. (B) The correct option is B, using the conjunction *and* to indicate inclusion.

353. (C) This is the best option to clearly indicate how that percentage of the working age population is making the most of its money.

354. (C) The correct answer is C to maintain subject–verb agreement.

355. (B) The best option is after sentence 2 because it introduces the topics a potential driver needs to consider.

356. (D) This option best improves the flow and clarity of the sentence by using a single subject and verb.

357. (A) No change is necessary.

358. (C) This option would most improve the underlines sentence because it clarifies what Uber does not do.

359. (C) *When* is the best option because the sentence relates to time.

360. (B) The correct choice is *your* to indicate possession.

361. (B) This is the best option because the graph refers to *gross* earnings.

362. (C) This information would best fit paragraph 4, which discusses income and earnings.

363. (A) This is the best option because the graph lacks information that would determine how well it supports the passage.

Passage 9

364. (D) This option is the correct verb tense for the sentence.

365. (C) The best vocabulary option is *evokes,* meaning "creates a feeling."

366. (A) This option provides the most logical reasoning because the information has already been stated.

367. (D) This option uses correct punctuation.

368. (C) This is the best option because it states the most important piece of information first in the comparison.

369. (C) *Raised* is the best vocabulary option because it best fits the purpose of a charity event.

370. (B) *Inspire* is the best option to maintain appropriate verb tense.

371. (D) This option best corrects the run-on sentence by clarifying cause and effect.

372. (C) The correct option is *them* to maintain pronoun–antecedent agreement.

373. (B) Paragraph 3 would be the most logical choice because it discusses other Banksy events and accomplishments.

Passage 10

374. (D) This option correctly uses punctuation to connect the two complete sentences.

375. (C) This is the correct option because *that* indicates a restrictive clause necessary to describe the contents of the letter.

376. (C) This option most effectively combines the two sentences without being repetitive.

377. (A) No change necessary.

378. (D) This is the most logical option because World War II occurs chronologically after the other events mentioned.

379. (A) No change is necessary. This is the best vocabulary option.

380. (B) The best option is *if* because *whether* is used with two alternatives or a comparison.

381. (B) *Societies* is the appropriate spelling for the plural form of the word.

382. (D) This is the correct option to maintain pronoun–antecedent agreement.

383. (B) Statistics showing an increase in profits from sporting and recreational businesses during daylight savings time would best support arguments made in paragraph 4 because that is specifically mentioned as being a positive outcome.

384. (B) This option is correct. The sentence should not be deleted because it concludes there is no definitive answer for the impact of daylights savings time on society.

Passage 11

385. (C) *Appeared* is the best option because the action is past tense.

386. (A) No change is necessary.

387. (D) *Try* is the best option to maintain the correct verb tense.

388. (D) *Sustain* is the best option because it refers to keeping the movie going for two hours.

389. (B) The best option is B because it specifies reasons the material would be inappropriate.

390. (A) No change is necessary.

391. (C) Option C best revises the underlined sentences by simplifying the subject of the sentence and the list of items.

392. (C) The best option is C.

393. (B) Option B uses correct punctuation.

394. (C) Option C best replaces the underlined words because it allows for a positive or negative impact.

395. (A) The most logical placement is after sentence 1 because the following sentence gives a specific example of something out of the author's control.

Passage 12

396. (B) *Conjures* is the correct verb form to maintain subject–verb agreement.

397. (B) *They're* is the correct option, meaning "they are."

398. (C) *Consuming* is the best option because the fish are eating the food.

399. (A) The most logical placement is after sentence 2 because it gives a specific example of the dangers related to the size of the fish previously stated.

400. (A) No change is necessary.

401. (D) This option makes the most sense to add because it details the effectiveness of methods discussed in the paragraph.

402. (B) Option B correctly uses a comma to separate two complete sentences with a conjunction.

403. (B) The correct option is *its*, indicating possession.

404. (D) *Sustains* is the correct choice because it means "to support continuously."

405. (B) The states most at risk are along the Mississippi River.

406. (C) The information would best support paragraph 3, which discusses how much money has been spent on efforts to prevent the spread of the fish.

407. (C) The author would most likely agree with statement C.

Passage 13

408. (C) The best option is *indigenous* because it means "native to."

409. (C) The correct option is *have* to maintain subject–verb agreement.

410. (C) The correct option is C to maintain correct comma use between two complete sentences with a conjunction.

411. (B) The best option is after sentence 4 because it specifies when the skulls should be dug up and the previous sentence describe their beliefs about the skulls when they are buried.

412. (B) The best option is after the word *dressed* because it describes what the skulls are dressed in.

413. (B) The best option is *volatile* because it means "unpredictable and inconsistent."

414. (B) The best option is *refused* to indicate past tense.

415. (B) B is the best option with the most logical explanation.

416. (A) No change is necessary.

417. (C) The correct choice is *is* to maintain subject–verb agreement.

Passage 14

418. (A) No change is necessary because *epitome* means "the essence" of something.

419. (B) Option B is correct because it offers the most logical reason.

420. (A) No change is necessary.

421. (C) The correct option is *everyone* because it is inclusive.

422. (C) Option C best reconciles the punctuation errors.

423. (D) The correct option is *thinks* because the action is present tense.

424. (C) The correct option is *of* because it indicates the context of the events.

425. (B) Option B is correct because it indicates cause and effect.

426. (A) Option A is the best option because the sentence introduces the idea of alternative attractions to visit.

427. (B) B is the best option because you would use a colon to indicate a list.

428. (B) The correct option is B because *remnants* means "the remains" of something.

429. (C) The correct option is C because the history will not be forgotten.

430. (B) Adding a paragraph about the Grand Canyon would be the most logical choice because the passage discusses other natural attractions in relation to the location to the Grand Canyon.

Passage 15

431. (B) The correct option is B because the sentence is redundant.

432. (B) Option B uses the correct punctuation to separate a descriptive phrase from the rest of the sentence.

433. (D) The correct option is D because the action is past tense.

434. (C) The correct option is C because a comma is not needed if there are not two complete sentences.

435. (C) *Discourage* is the best vocabulary option to indicate that Disney's attitude remained positive.

436. (A) No change is necessary.

437. (B) The correct preposition to use is *in*.

438. (C) The most logical placement would be after sentence 3 because it explains what cartoons were filmed.

439. (B) The correct verb tense is *opened*.

440. (B) The best option for revising the underlined portion is B.

Passage 16

441. (A) The best option is A.

442. (A) No change necessary.

443. (C) Option C uses punctuation correctly to combine two complete sentences using a conjunction.

444. (C) The best location for the sentence would be after sentence 5 because it specifically refers to the age of trade workers.

445. (B) The best option is *remain* because it indicates the positions continue to be unfilled.

446. (B) *Most* is the best option because evidence can be found to support the claims, but it is not universal.

447. (A) The most logical location for the underlined sentence is to move it to paragraph 3 to maintain a consistent topic.

448. (B) The best option is *had* because it refers to information from past census information.

449. (C) This is the best option because *corresponds with* means the education would be linked to or parallel their career.

450. (C) This option provides a stronger conclusion summarizing the importance of the information in the passage.

Passage 17

451. **(B)** Option B uses correct punctuation.

452. **(C)** *Means* is the best option to maintain appropriate verb tense.

453. **(D)** Option D offers the best revision of the underlined phrase.

454. **(D)** *Was* is the best option to maintain appropriate verb tense.

455. **(C)** Option C correctly uses the apostrophe to indicate plural possession.

456. **(B)** Option B is correct. No comma is necessary to combine the complete sentence with the dependent clause.

457. **(D)** D is the best option to revise the underlined sentences.

458. **(A)** No change is necessary.

459. **(B)** B is the correct option because 2 of the 4 squares have the capital B to indicate a dominant gene.

460. **(B)** B is the correct answer because 2 of the 4 squares have two bs, indicating recessive blue eyes.

461. **(A)** Paragraph 2 would most benefit from the information presented in the graphic to illustrate how dominant and recessive genes are manifested.

Passage 18

462. **(D)** The underlined phrase can be deleted because the detail is irrelevant to the passage.

463. **(A)** No change is necessary.

464. **(B)** *Convinced* is the correct option to maintain appropriate verb tense.

465. **(B)** Option B offers the best revision for the underlined sentence.

466. **(B)** Option B correctly uses the comma with a conjunction.

467. **(A)** No change is necessary.

468. **(D)** The most appropriate conjunction is *and* because the statements do not contradict each other.

469. (C) The most logical placement for the sentence is after sentence 4 because it gives specific examples of DaVinci's knowledge.

470. (A) No change is necessary.

Passage 19

471. (A) No change necessary.

472. (B) The correct option is *it's* to mean "it is."

473. (C) Option C uses the correct punctuation to join two complete sentences with a comma and a conjunction.

474. (B) *Could* is the best option because it indicates a problem is possible, but not definite.

475. (D) *Offer* is the best option to maintain subject–verb agreement.

476. (B) Paragraph 3 is the most logical place to add the sentence because it discusses the ideal conditions for off-grid living in relation to the options being considered by the narrator.

477. (C) "More primitive living" is the best option.

478. (A) The best place to divide the underlined sentence is between *systems* and *land* because both parts can stand alone as complete sentences.

479. (B) Option B offer the best revision for clarity.

480. (C) "Is cheapest" is the best option because it is a singular subject, and the next sentence says "most affordable," indicating there is nothing cheaper.

Passage 20

481. (B) The best option is *is* because it is a singular subject.

482. (C) This is the best option because no comma is necessary between two verb phrases when there is only one subject.

483. (D) *Blame* is the appropriate choice to maintain subject–verb agreement.

484. (A) No change is necessary.

485. (B) Option B uses the correct spelling of *presence*.

486. (C) *Was* is the correct choice to maintain subject–verb agreement.

487. (B) The most logical placement is after sentence 2 because it can date when the Polynesians arrived in Hawaii.

488. (A) Option A provides the most logical reason for deleting the underlined sentence.

489. (C) *Is* correctly maintains subject–verb agreement.

490. (B) *It* correctly maintains pronoun–antecedent agreement.

Passage 21

491. (C) *Grew* would be the correct verb tense to indicate past growth.

492. (B) Option B provides the best revision of the underlined phrase.

493. (B) *Told* maintains a consistent use of past tense throughout the sentence.

494. (A) *And* is the best option to combine the two sentences because both sentences include reasons for Dannon's success.

495. (D) *Marketed* is the best option because it means "promoted or advertised."

496. (C) This is the best option because a comma is needed to set apart a nonessential phrase.

497. (A) No change is necessary.

498. (B) The best option is to delete the underlined words completely because they are unnecessary.

499. (D) Paragraph 5 is the best location to insert the sentence because it discusses the various new roles of yogurt that appeal to the convenience factor mentioned in the paragraph.

500. (B) B is the best option to create one complete sentence.